Little Annie's ART Book of Etiquette & Good Manners

by
Barry & Saundra Stebbing

Little Annie's
ART Book
of
Etiquette & Good Manners
by
Barry & Saundra Stebbing

Copyright First Edition 1995
Second Edition 2004
Published by How Great Thou ART Publications
(Lessons within Annie's Art Book are reproducible for "in house" use only.)

"You prepare a table before me...." Psalm 23:5

Setting
The Table of Contents

Listed below is the table of contents, served to you just as the courses of a dinner:

Serving the Hors d'oeuvres
Chapter One:…………Peers……………Page 7
Serving the Appetizer
Chapter Two:………… Guests…………Page 35
Serving the Salad
Chapter Three…………Family…………Page 49
Serving the Entree
Chapter Four:…………Elders…………Page 73
Serving the Vegetables
Chapter Five:…………Cut & Paste……Page 83
Serving the Dessert
Chapter Six:………Colored Markers…Page 105

"Teach a child to choose the right path, and when he is older he will remain upon it."   Proverbs 22:6

This book is dedicated to all the well mannered home schooled children we have met across America.

"Teaching your children manners is also teaching them values, ethics, and morals. A child's character develops and is shaped through their own life experiences and through the influence and teaching of other people, especially those whom they are close to and love. In the best of worlds, parents and children should be polite to each other more than to anyone else."
      Letitia Baldrige, *The New Manners of the 90's*

The Golden Rule
"Love Your Neighbor As Yourself."
Mark 12:31

The 2nd Commandment sums up all the good rules of etiquette, manners and politeness. To simplify, all we need to do is treat everyone as if they are very special. We should always show love, kindness and respect to others. Little Annie is going to be our role model for this book of etiquette. So have your art materials ready and let's learn God's way to good manners.

"Hello. My name is Annie. I will be your hostess for the entire book. So, bring along your colored pencils, scissors and glue and follow me, please."

"All ten (commandments) are wrapped up in this one, to love your neighbor as you love yourself." Romans 13:9

"Parents who read Bible stories every night to their children, explaining the moral lessons contained in those pages, instill a respect not only for God but for other human beings in the hearts of their children. A respect for God and for other human beings is, after all, the foundation of manners, morals, ethics and values."
    Letitia Baldrige

Peers

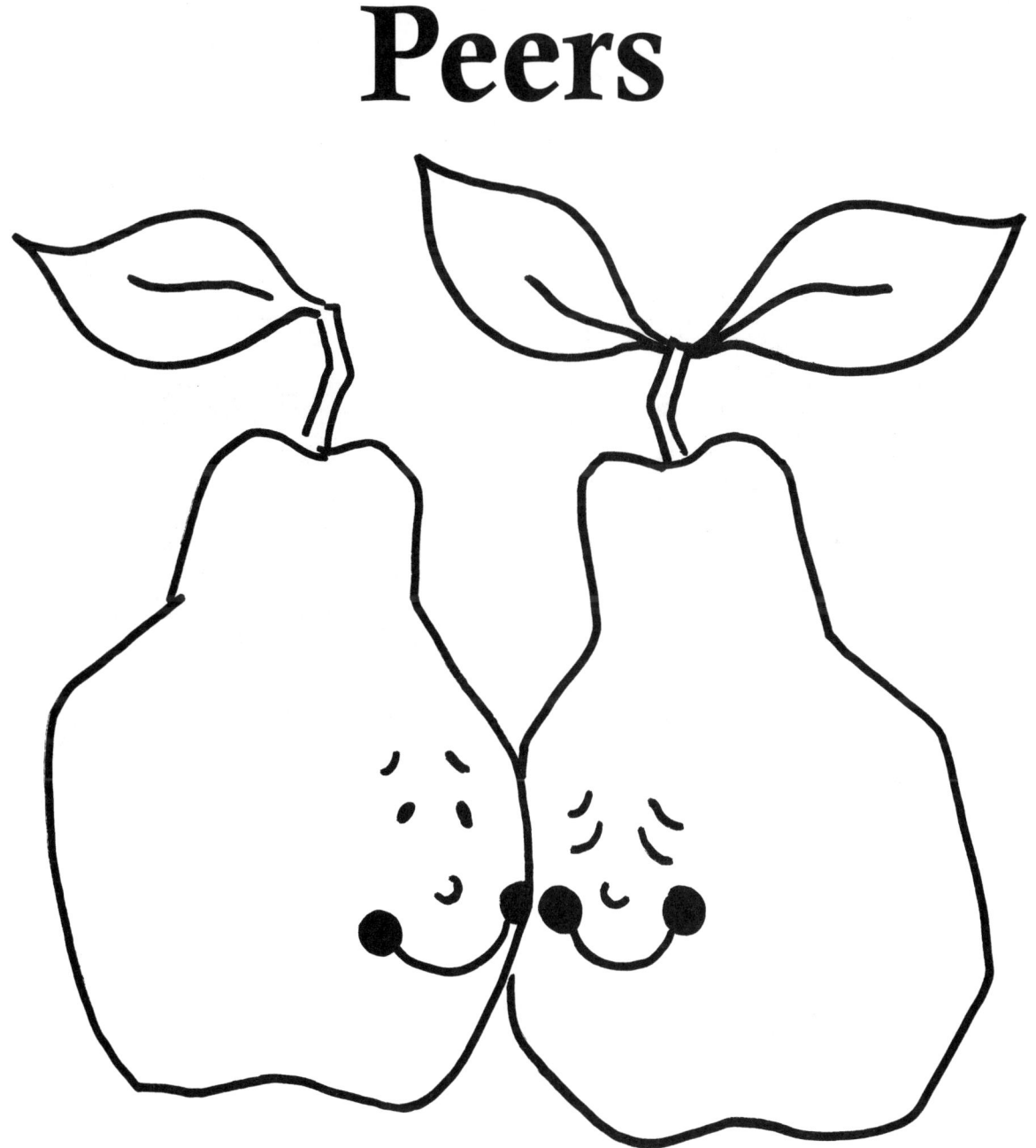

A friend loves at all times."   Proverbs 17:17

"Tis better to be alone, than in bad company." George Washington

Friendship

Peers are not pears! A peer is a person who has the same standing with another, such as the same age, the same grade, and so forth. Your friends are generally considered your peers. Peers can be a good influence or a bad influence on you. But what's more important is that you can be a good influence on them, especially by using etiquette and good manners.

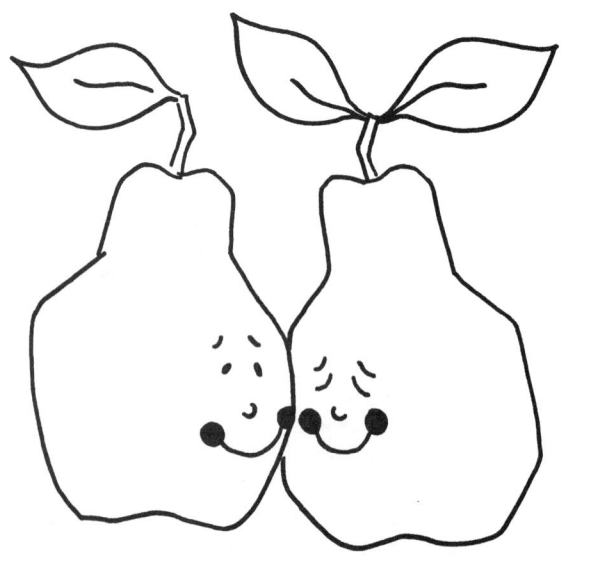 

Assignment: Draw and color two pears. Put funny faces on them. When finished, color them in with your yellow and green colored pencils.

Peers: Your friends.

"A person who shows himself friendly will have many friends."
Proverbs 18:24

Little Miss Annie
Can you draw Annie in the picture box (left)? When you are finished, color the picture with your primary colors: Red, Yellow and Blue.

Annie has many friends. Do you know why? Because she has the wonderful quality of being nice to others. Everyone likes Annie because she is kind and courteous. Remember, people are attracted to gracious people.

Gracious: Being kind and courteous to others.

"Never abandon a friend......."   **Proverbs 27:10**

*"Make new friends and keep the old,
one is silver and the other is gold."*

Friend #1	Friend #2
My name is: _____	My name is: _____

    Annie is always certain to introduce her new friends to everyone. Please, make new friends feel right at home. Treat them extra special around your other friends, making sure to introduce them to everyone!

Assignment: Can you draw and color two more friends on this page for Annie? What are their names? What do they like to do? Can you write 25 words or more about each friend describing their personalities? Your parent or teacher can help with writing this assignment if you need assistance.

"Bad company corrupts good morals."   I Corinthians 15:33

Overlapping

See if you can overlap the balloons. Overlapping means placing one in front of another.

Warm Colors:
Red
Yellow
Orange

Cool Colors:
Blue
Green
Violet

    Annie's peers like her. Do you know why? Because she is always pleasant to them. Some of Annie's friends are very well-behaved and some are not well-behaved. Are you well-behaved? Can you draw and color 3 balloons in each of Annie's hands? Then, draw a happy face on 3 of them and a sad face on the other 3. Color the happy faces with warm colors and the sad faces with cool colors.

"A cheerful look brings joy to the heart." **Proverbs 15:30**

We have told you that some of Annie's friends are not nice all of the time. Sometimes they may become moody. Their personalities might change to: pouty, whiny, angry, stubborn and so on. Look at the six faces below. Do you know what their moods are? Are they excited, angry, pouty, happy, stubborn or pleasant? Write the word that best describes them underneath each face.

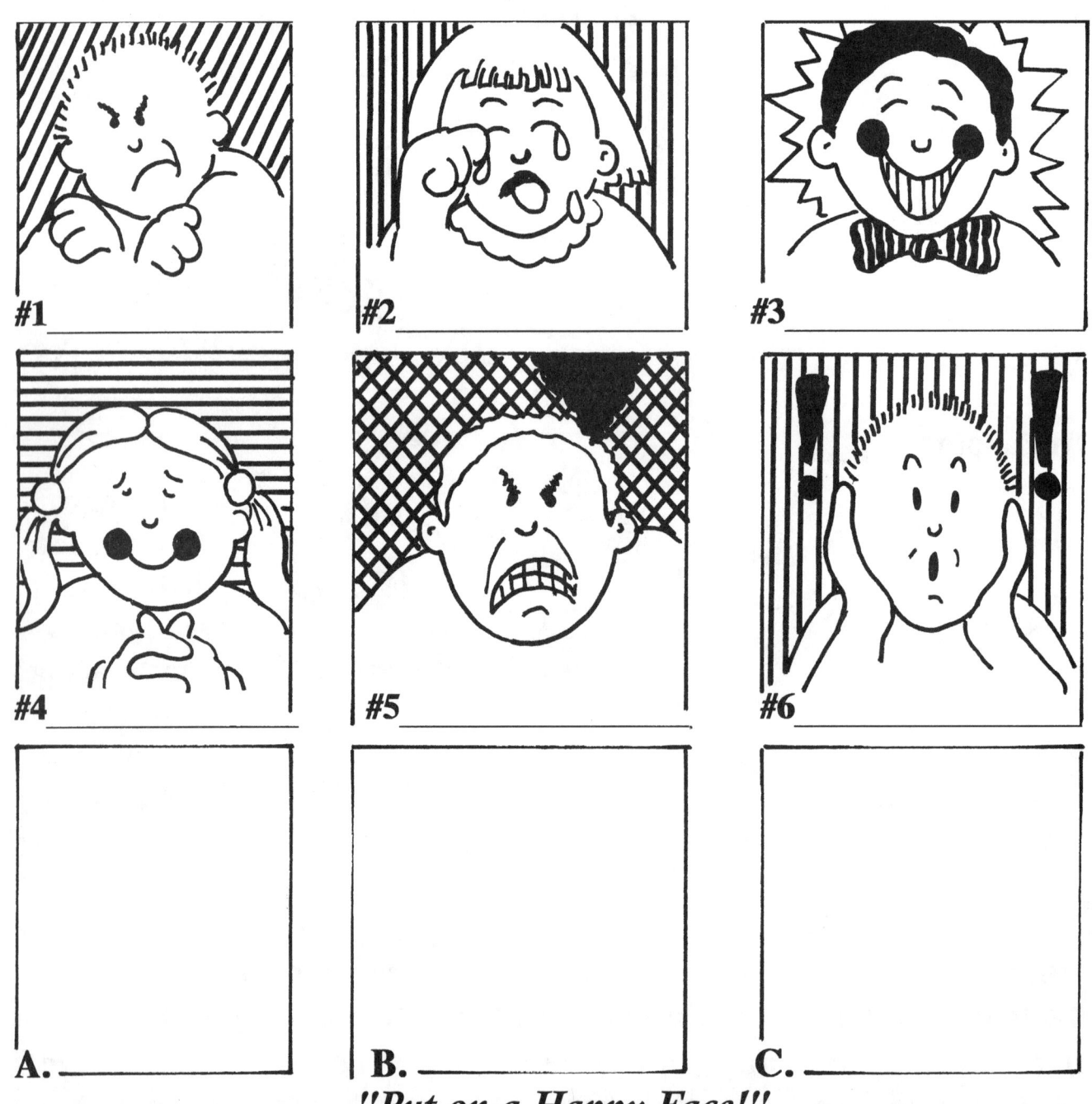

"Put on a Happy Face!"

Annie's desire is to always have a pleasant personality. However, some of her best friends let their feelings show on their faces. Can you draw three faces above in A, B and C. Give each face a different mood.

"Be quick to listen and slow to speak." James 1:19

Annie is always *courteous* when she is in the company of others. She is a good listener and never interrupts when someone is talking.

Assignment: In the picture above, can you draw some more trees in the background and then color everything? Can you draw and color some flowers around their picnic area?

Courteous: Being polite and considerate of others.

"How wonderful it is to be able to say the right thing at the right time!
Proverbs 15:23

Please   Etiquette   Thank You

There is a proper way and an improper way to do things. Learning *etiquette* will teach you proper manners and procedures for doing everything in a pleasing way when dealing with other people.

Assignment: Can you letter? See if you can letter the words *"Please," "Etiquette,"* and *"Thank You"* on the guidelines above, letting the top and bottom of each letter touch the lines. Then, color in the picture above.

Etiquette: The proper way to do things.

"A happy heart makes the face cheerful." **Proverbs 15:13**

Did you know that just by smiling you can make your friends smile? We should all practice smiling more often, especially around others!

Place Your Smiling Face Here ➤

"When you're smiling, the whole world smiles with you."

Assignment:

Look in a mirror with the biggest, warmest smile you have. Draw your smiling face in the picture frame above. Your drawing is probably going to make you smile even more than you're smiling now.

"My command is this: Love each other as I have loved you."

John 15:12

Cotton Relay Game

Annie likes to play with her friends. One fun game they like to play is the *Cotton Relay Game*.

Materials:
Spoons
Cotton Balls

Instructions:
1. Make a start and finish line.
2. Place the cotton ball in your spoon and, at the count of five, walk or run to the finish line.
3. If the cotton ball falls off the spoon you must return to the starting line and begin again.
4. The first one to pass the finish line is the winner!

GET ON YOUR MARK......

GET SET....

GO!

Assignment: Finish drawing the picture above by drawing a spoon and cotton ball in each of their hands. When you are finished, color the picture.

"If one falls down, his friend can help him up."

Ecclesiastes 4:10

"A friend in need is a friend indeed."

When Annie's friends are sad, she is always there to comfort them and to listen to their problems. Isn't that what friends are for ?

Assignment: Color the heart (above) bright red. Draw and color flowers around the bottom of the heart. Then turn to pages 86 and 87 and learn how to make a card for one of your friends. Using your colored pencils, color some flowers and hearts on the card and whatever else will make your friend happy. Save the card for when you have a friend that is sad. Let's also make our own stickers! Turn to page 85 and color the stickers. When you want to use them, simply cut them out and glue them on your cards and envelopes. Finally, turn to page 89 and learn how to make your own envelopes.

"Be humble, thinking of others as better than yourself. Don't just think about your own affairs, but be interested in others too, and what they are doing." **Philippians 2:3,4**

When Annie is with her friends she always tries to do what they want to do, not having her own way. If they are hungry, she will eat. If they want to play, she will play with them. If they want to go home, she will understand and say "Goodbye." Annie never puts herself above others.

My Favorite Foods

Square   Triangle   Circle   Rectangle

Assignment: What foods do you like to eat? Can you draw and color four of them around Annie in the geometric shapes? Geometric shapes are shapes such as squares, rectangles, circles and triangles.

"........always be thankful......" **I Thessalonians 5:18**

Receiving Presents

When Annie receives a present she is always grateful, no matter how small the gift. She takes her time opening a present. First she looks at the card and shows it to everyone and then says, "Thank You." Then she pauses and looks at the wrapped gift, taking the time to appreciate and compliment the fine wrapping. Finally, she slowly unwraps the present, taking care not to quickly and carelessly rip the wrapping paper. When Annie opens it, she is not only surprised but sincerely thankful for the thoughtfulness that her friend or family member had in taking the time and expense to give her the gift. Then, Annie gives her friend a big hug and another warm "Thank You!" Last of all, she picks up the wrapping paper and gift and places them neatly aside.

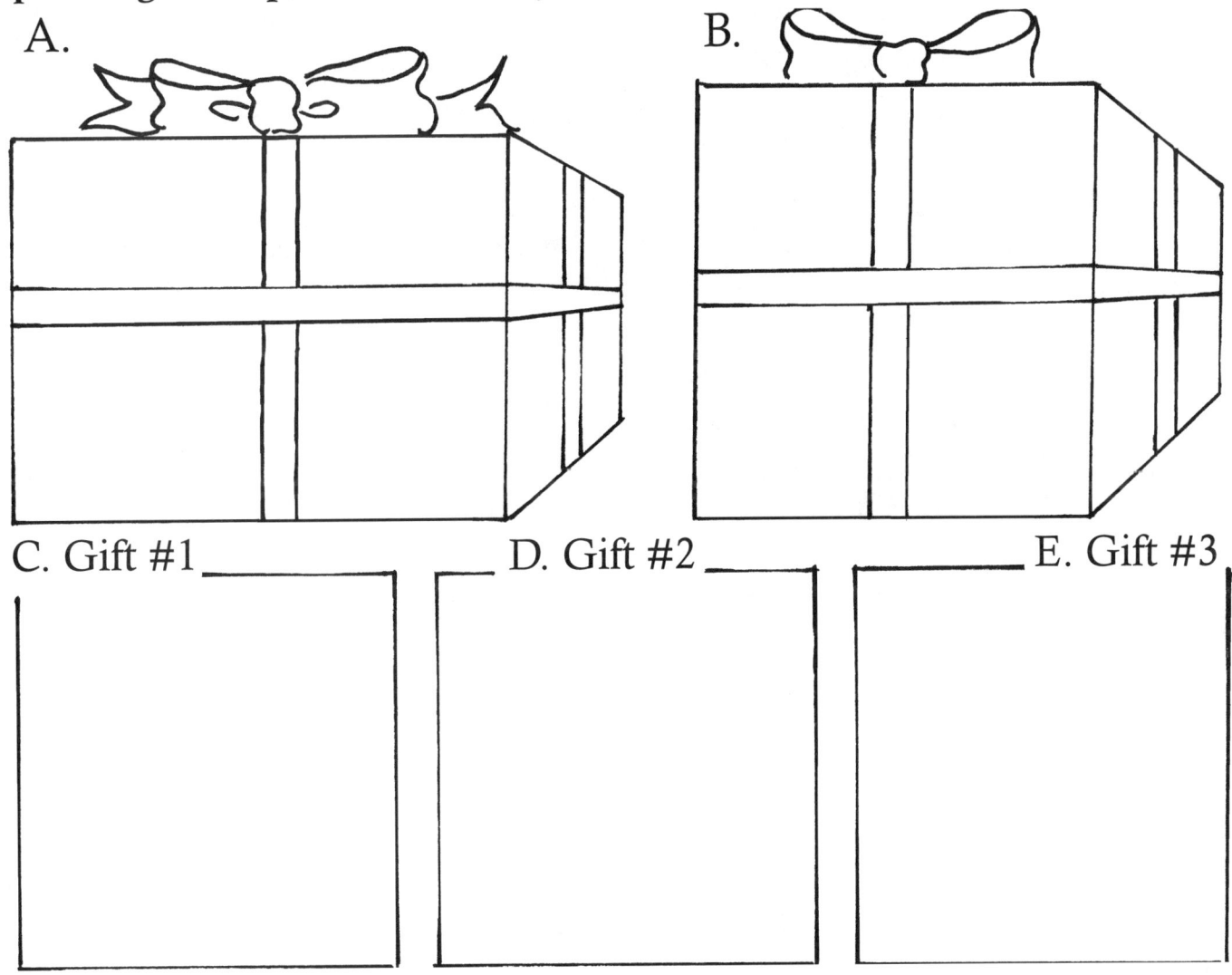

A.   B.   C. Gift #1   D. Gift #2   E. Gift #3

Assignment: Can you place some nice, colorful designs on the two packages above A & B with your colored pencils? Then, draw and color three gifts that you would like in the boxes above C, D and E.

19

Porcupines in the Box

Did you ever hear the story about the porcupines in the box? Well, the story goes like this....."Once upon a time, on a cold and wintry day, there were several porcupines stranded out in the snow. They were very cold and had no where to go to keep warm. Finally, they came upon and large box and scurried inside. "Br-r-r-r-r-r, it's cold out!" One of the porcupines said as he shook off the snow. One by one, the other porcupines entered the box. Now this was a very large box and there were only a few porcupines, so even though it was warmer inside than outside, it was still very cold. So they scurried to the middle of the box and huddled together for warmth. But no sooner had they come together then they would prick each other. "Ouch!" they would cry, scurrying once again to the far corners of the box. Well, in a little while they would become cold again and their teeth would begin to chatter. Quickly they would scurry to the center of the box to keep each other warm only to prick each other again and hastily return to the far walls. So it went, back and forth, and back and forth scurried the porcupines. And that's the story of the porcupines in the box, needing each other for warmth but when they got too close they would hurt each other and scurry away. Does that sound familiar? Don't you think that we are like this with some of our friends?

How To Make a Box

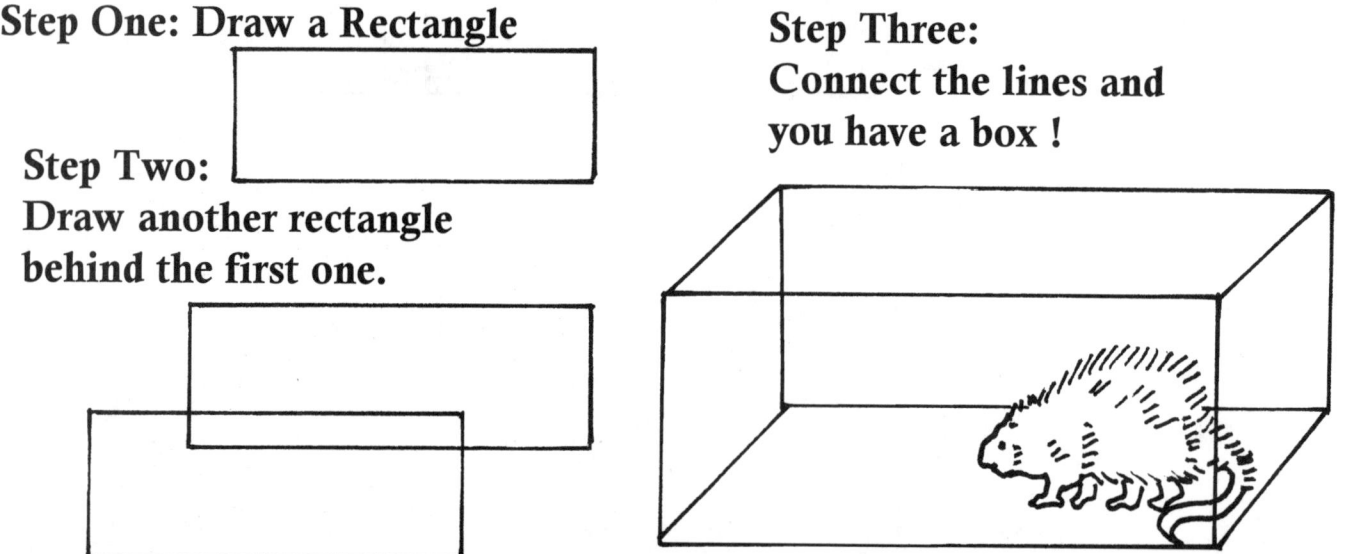

Step One: Draw a Rectangle

Step Two: Draw another rectangle behind the first one.

Step Three: Connect the lines and you have a box !

Assignment: Do you know how to draw a box? See if you can draw a big box on the next page and place some porcupines in it. Have fun drawing the porcupines. Make them fat and fluffy with long quills coming out of their hairy coat. Give them funny, cartoon faces.

Porcupines in a Box

↑
Place Box Here

"Be beautiful inside, in your hearts, with.... a gentle and quiet spirit which is so precious to God." I Peter 3:4

What Are You Thinking About? Pretend you are sitting at a table with Annie and her friends. Draw and color a picture of what you would like to draw if you were with Annie doing artwork. Do you think she would like your drawing?

Annie is always pleasant. Whenever she plays with her friends she is polite and friendly. She is never pushy, pouty or wanting her own way. If she is borrowing her friend's crayons she takes very special care of them and returns them neatly in the box. When she returns them she sincerely says, "Thank you, very much!"

"I praise you because I am fearfully and wonderfully made."
Psalm 139:14

Assignment: Can you draw your hand with a colored pencil in A? Then, draw Annie's hands in B.

A. My Hand by_____

B. Annie's Hands

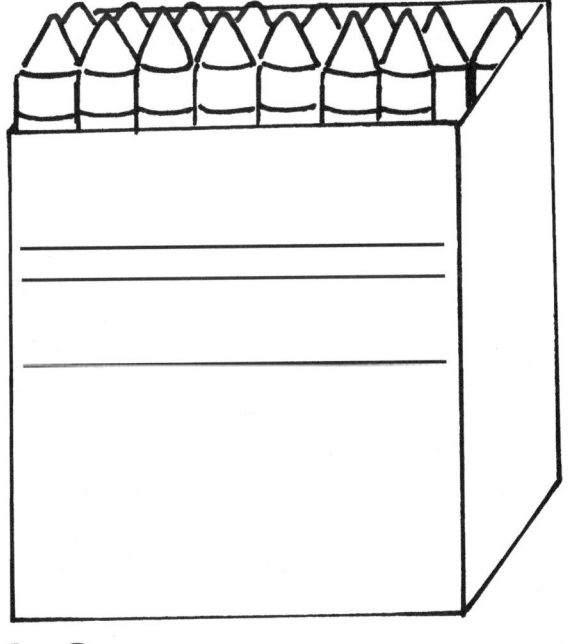

C. Crayons

D.

Remember how we learned to draw a box on page 20? Let's see if you can make a crayon box. Copy the box in D, place crayons in the box and then place the word "Crayons" on the box. Before beginning see if you can letter "Crayons" on the box in C.

"In the end, people appreciate frankness more than flattery."

Proverbs 28:23

A.

"Bo-Bo"

B.

Flattery......................or ....Compliments?

☐	"My, Bo-Bo, that shirt fits you so nicely!"	☐
☐	"My, Bo-Bo, what beautiful flowers!"	☐
☐	"Oh, Bo-Bo, you look so thin!"	☐
☐	"Bo-Bo, I love your bright smile!"	☐
☐	"Bo-Bo, you are such a neat dresser!"	☐

To *"flatter"* is much different than to *"compliment."* It is not good to give someone false flattery, which is like giving praise when it is not deserved. However, it is very good to praise someone for good qualities.

Assignment:
Look at *"Bo-Bo"* above. Select from the list of statements which are flattery and the statements which are sincere compliments. Draw another person next to *"Bo-Bo"* in B and give him or her some very good qualities. He may have a nice smile, or a nice tie, or nice hair. Ask your parents what they like about your person and see if they can praise those good qualities.

Flattery: Insincere praise.

"God loves colors. The Bible says, "A rainbow....encircled His throne."

Revelations 4:3

A. COLOR WHEEL   **B. Complementary Colors**

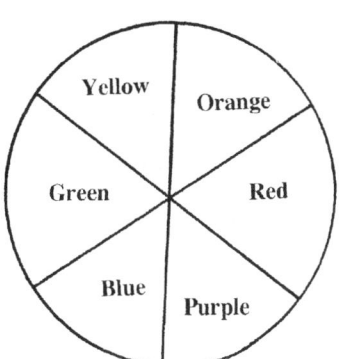

1. The complement of red is _____.
2. The complement of blue is _____.
3. The complement of yellow is _____.
4. The complement of orange is _____.
5. The complement of violet is _____.
6. The complement of green is _____.

C.

D.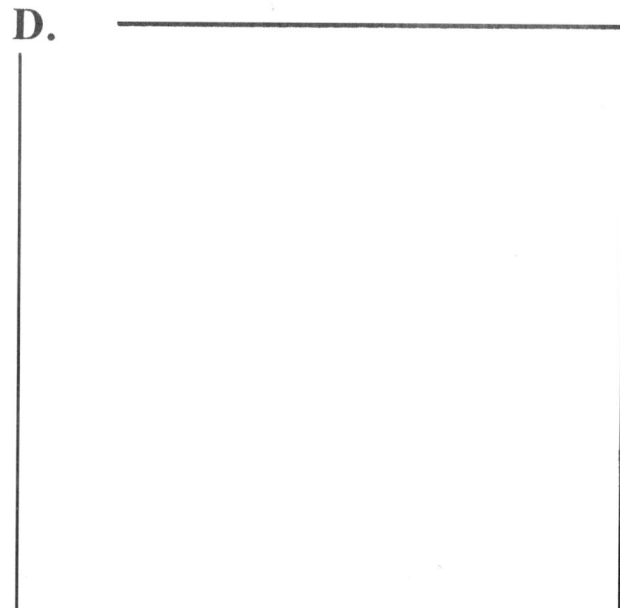

A complement in art is the color which is on the opposite side of another color on the color wheel. For instance, the complement of red is green, the complement of blue is orange, and the complement of yellow is violet. Why? Because they are opposite each other on the color wheel. Complementary colors are great to use when coloring just as compliments are great to use with people!

Assignment: Color the color wheel above (A) and fill in the blanks in (B). Next, color the little patterns in C with complementary colors. Color one with red and its complement (green), another with orange and its complement (blue), another with yellow and its complement (violet) and so forth. Then in D, see if you can make some simple designs and color them with "complementary colors."

Compliment: An admiring remark.
Complement: An opposite color on the color wheel.

"Do what is right." I Peter 3:16

"Gimme that!" "Let's do it my way!" "That's mine!"

Whiny Winnie

Color Wheel

Do you have friends who seem to always want to have their own way? They pout or whine if they don't get what they want. They say, "I want that, gimme-e-e" or "That's mine!" Try not to argue with such children, but continue to be a good example around them, showing them the best of your manners.

A. Sad Clown: Cool Colors

B. Happy Clown: Warm Colors

Assignment: Color in the colors in the color wheel above. Do you remember the warm and cool colors you learned on page 11? Warm colors are red, orange and yellow. Warm colors seem to be happy and bright! The cool colors are blue, green and violet. Cool colors seem sad and gloomy. Can you color Whiny Winnie with cool colors? Then, color the clowns above. Color the sad clown with cool colors and the happy clown with warm colors!

"Don't repay evil for evil. Don't snap back at those who say unkind things about you. Instead, pray for God's help for them, for we are to be kind to others, and God will bless us for it." **I Peter 3:9**

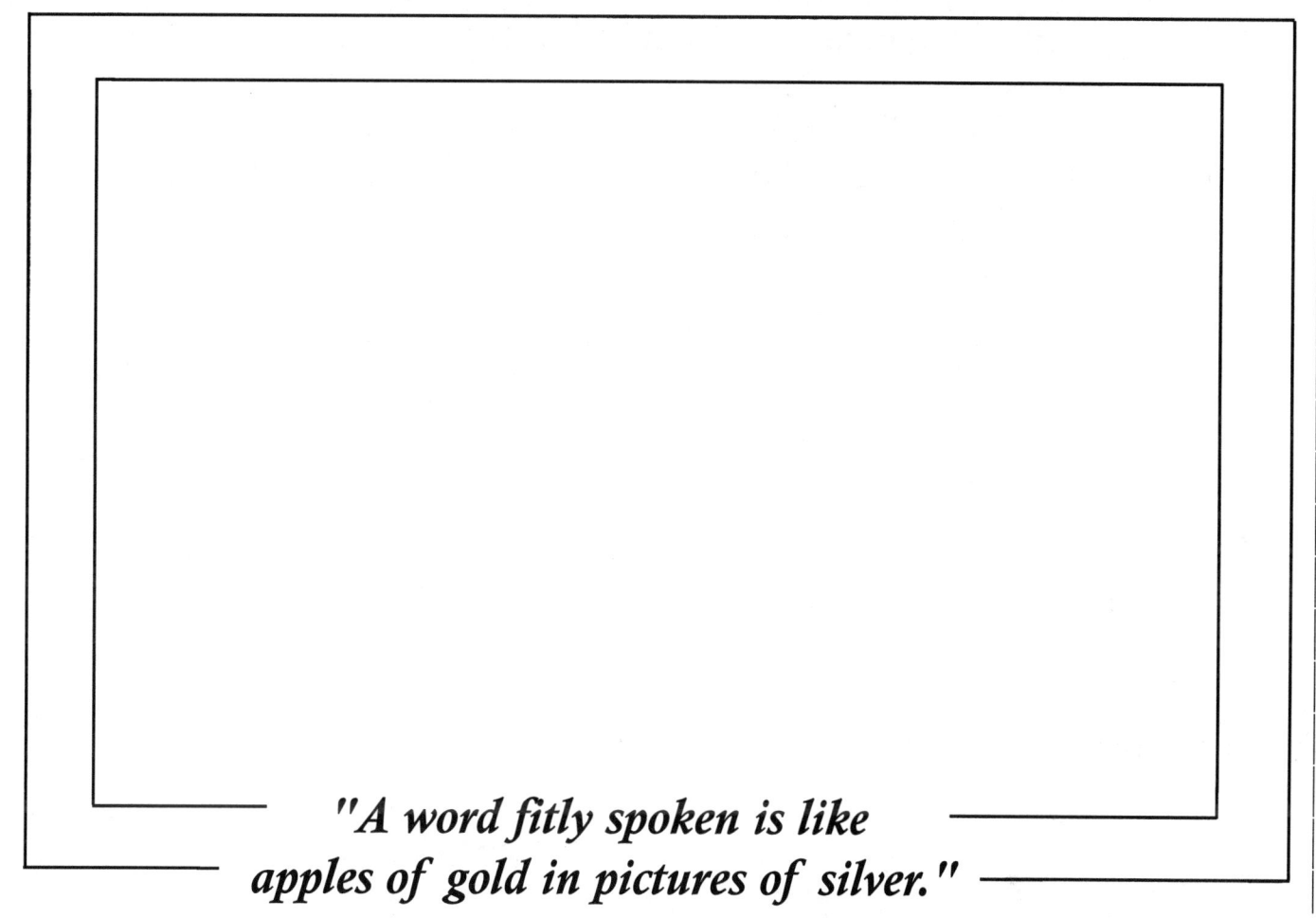

"A word fitly spoken is like apples of gold in pictures of silver."

Proverbs 25:11

What do you do when someone is <u>unkind</u> to you, or when one of your friends has said something that really hurts you? Have you ever tried saying something nice in return? Remember, it takes two people to have an argument. When you decide to be nice and return soft, pleasant words, you will be surprised at what happens!

Assignment: Can you draw a "still life?" A still life is a composition of objects which do not move when you are drawing them. Objects like these are easy to study and draw. Set up three apples and draw and color them in the big frame above. Study the apples and see how many other colors you see in them besides red. Place one apple a little bit in front of another so you can practice "overlapping" just as we learned with the balloons on page 11. Color the background with the complementary color of red. Last of all, decorate the frame around your apples.

"And be thankful." **Colossians 3:15**

Spending the Night Over

When spending the night at a friend's house, you should not decide you want to go home just because you're homesick, but enjoy this special time together. During your stay, do not be disruptive or messy, and take special care of their belongings. When it is time to go to bed, make sure you are quiet, being respectful of others. The next morning you may want to help with making the beds and cleaning up. The only thing that Annie leaves behind is a good impression.

"When home is ruled according to God's Word, angels might be asked to stay with us, and they would not find themselves out of their element." Charles Spurgeon

Assignment: Do you ever have wonderful dreams? Do you remember the dreams Joseph and Daniel had in the Bible? They were really exciting! Draw and color one of your dreams above. Show it to your friends and see if they can guess what you were dreaming about. Then, turn to page 90 and make a thank you card for your friend, and mail it to your friend in appreciation of their wonderful hospitality.

"Do not take the seat of honor....but take the lowest place....when your host comes, he will say to you, 'Friend, move up to a better place.' Then you will be honored in front of all the other guests." Luke 14:8,10

A. Side View

B. Front View

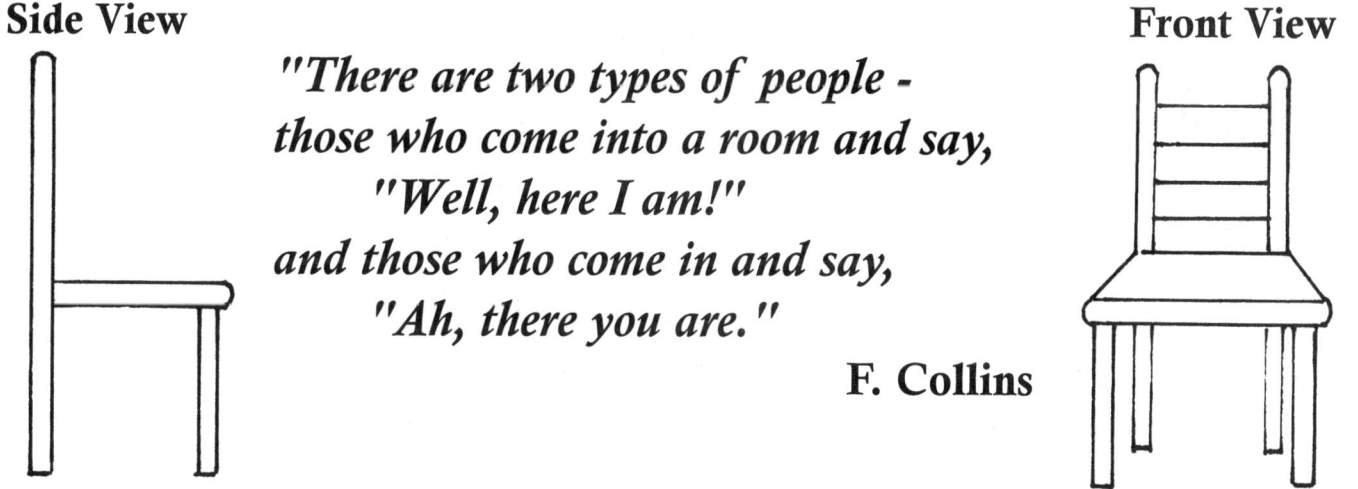

"There are two types of people - those who come into a room and say, "Well, here I am!" and those who come in and say, "Ah, there you are."

F. Collins

Annie is never the center of attention. When she is playing with her friends, she tries to do what they want to do by paying attention to them and treating everyone with respect. That is why her friends and their parents like her so much and always give her a special seat during dinner.

Assignment: Can you draw a chair with someone sitting in it from the side view (A) and from the front view (B)?

"For the Lord is watching His children, listening to their prayers."
                                                                    I Peter 3:12

Making & Playing Games at Home

Have you ever made games with your friends? This can be a lot of fun. Let's make a game and play it with our friends the next time we visit them.

12 Steps to Heaven

You will need:
- 1 egg carton
- 1 colored marker
- scissors
- a different pebble for each player (or button or bottle cap)
- paper for scorecard

Instructions:
1. Cut the top off an egg carton.
2. With colored marker, number the sections in the egg carton as shown.
3. Write the name of each player on your scorecard paper.
4. Place the egg carton about 12" from a mark on the floor.
5. Each player takes a turn to toss the button or pebble into the egg carton.
6. Keep score, and the first person to make 50 points is the winner.

Dots & Squares

Dots and Squares is a thinking game that can be played by two or more people. Annie likes to play this game on long car trips.

Materials: A.   B.
- paper   - pencil
- ruler   - marking pen

Rules:

1. Use the ruler and pencil to make rows of dots about 1/2" apart as shown in example A.
2. The players take turns connecting 2 dots with a marking pen. The dots can be connected by a line that goes up, down or across.
3. When a player completes a square, he or she writes their initial inside the new square and takes another turn as shown in B.
4. When all the dots are connected the game is over. The player whose initials are in the most squares wins the game.

C.

Whenever Annie spends the night with friends she loves to play games. Annie is always a good sport. If she wins she is gracious, having a good nature and gentle spirit, not bragging about how well she played. Annie has fun even if she loses and congratulates the winner! Win or lose she always helps to put the games away in their proper place.

Assignment: Follow the instructions above and let's play! Use the space above in C to prepare your first game of *Dots & Squares*.

"You must not be envious." Exodus 20:17

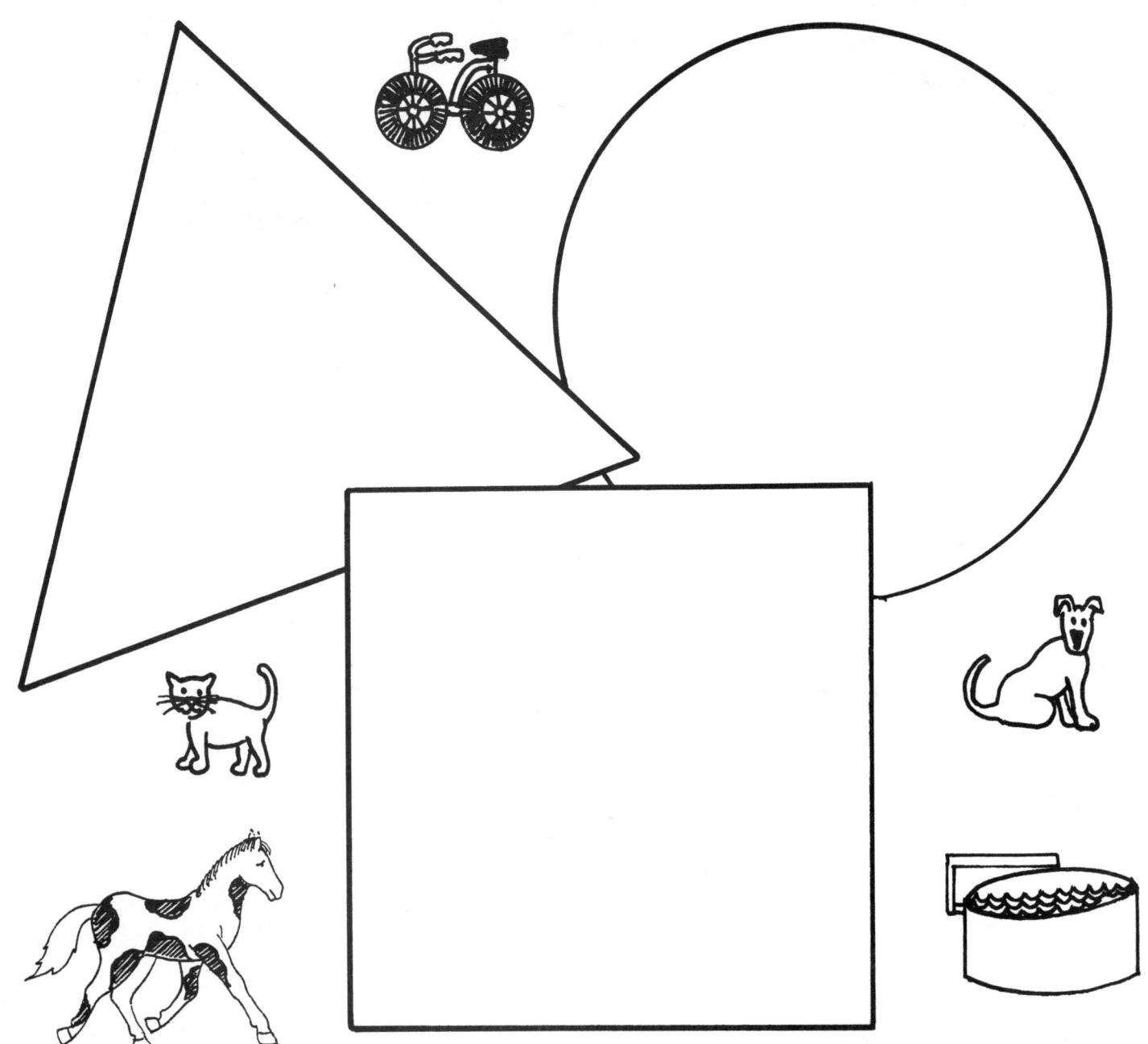

Annie never boasts or brags. She never says, *"My house is bigger than yours,"* or *"We have a swimming pool at our house,"* or *"I have a prettier doll than you have!"* Annie knows not to boast because it makes others uncomfortable and can make them feel not as worthy. Annie compliments the nice things her friends have.

Assignment: What three things would you like to have? A horse? A bicycle? A swimming pool? A cat or a dog? Can you draw and color them above, placing one in each of the geometric shapes: the triangle, the circle and the square?

Envy: To desire what belongs to another.

"We write this to make our joy complete." I John 1:4

Writing Friends

Annie does not *procrastinate!* When she receives a letter from a friend, she quickly responds with a return letter. It is good etiquette to reply to a letter as soon as possible. Annie likes to write her friends. The first thing she asks when writing a letter is how they are and what they have been doing? She shows an interest in them before writing about herself. Do you know what to write about in a letter? You can write about the weather, school, your artwork, or any interesting things that have happened to you recently.

Assignment: Write a letter to a friend. Can you color pretty decorations around it (see page 34)? Mail your letter as soon as possible. Do not procrastinate. Can you make an envelope (see page 89)? Color some nice decorations on your envelope also.

Procrastinate: To put off until tomorrow something that you should do today.

Charles Russell - American Artist

Charles Russell was a cowboy artist. When he was only 16 years of age he moved out west and lived with the cowboys and Indians. He loved the old West and enjoyed drawing and painting cowboys, horses, cattle, buffalo and Indians every opportunity he had. Almost all of his work was done on location and was very authentic. His artwork now gives us a wonderful history of the old West. He painted cowboys and Indians the way they were and showed the last of the great buffalo herds. He even painted wolves in the deep snows of winter. Whenever Charles Russell would write to his friends, he would draw or color something about the old West on the letters and envelopes. Just think what a treasure it was to receive an authentic drawing from a famous artist!

You never know. One day you may be as famous as Charles Russell and people will pull out the letters and envelopes you sent them and say, "This is what my friend did as a child."

Assignment: Go to the library and do a written report on Charles Russell. Practice penmanship in doing this assignment. Maybe your parents or older sister or brother can help you. What was your favorite painting by Charles Russell? Why? Would you like to paint like him when you grow up?

Penmanship: The art of writing with a pen;
beautiful writing.

"Practice hospitality." **Romans 12:13**

"They must enjoy having guests in their home and must love all that is good."

Titus 1:8

"Why, good evening Mr. and Mrs. Smith. Won't you please come in? May I take your coats?"

Mom's Little Helper

Can you draw and color the flowers in the vase on the table?

Welcome

Let's *practice hospitality!* When guests come to visit, practice being warm and friendly. Annie is going to be your *hostess* for the evening. Follow her as she *practices hospitality.*

Assignment: Draw and color flowers on the table in the foyer. Can you draw Annie's cat near the Welcome mat? Her cat is on page 63.

Hospitable: To be warm and friendly to guests.

Host/Hostess: A person who receives guests for a social visit.

"Offer hospitality to one another......" I Peter 4:9

A.

B.

C.

When Mr. and Mrs. Smith arrived for dinner, they brought their host a bouquet of flowers. This is done as a warm greeting to someone special and to show appreciation for the kind invitation.

Assignment: Draw a bouquet of flowers above (A). The first thing to do is draw circles to show where the flowers are going (B). See if you can *"overlap"* some of them. When drawing a flower, the stem goes up to the center of the flower as shown in C, and the petals come out from the center. Color your flowers with a burst of warm colors.

    Then, go outside and cut some small wildflowers and press them inside a heavy book. Leave them there for a long time (maybe a month). Then take them out and glue them to paper and make a thank you card (see pressed flowers, pages 76).

"But the fruit of the Spirit is love, joy, peace, patience, kindness, goodness, faithfulness, gentleness and self-control." Galatians 5:22

Feeding You Pets

It is a good habit to feed your pets before you eat. You have to understand that they are hungry too! Annie is aware of the needs of her pets and always feeds them before she sits down for dinner.

"Love is patient, love is kind." I Cor. 13:4

A. A Bird in the Cage   B. Dog on a Chain

C. Cat Near a Mouse   D. Fish in a Bowl

Assignment: Draw and color a bird in the cage (A), a dog on the chain (B), a cat near a mouse (C), and a fish in the bowl (D).

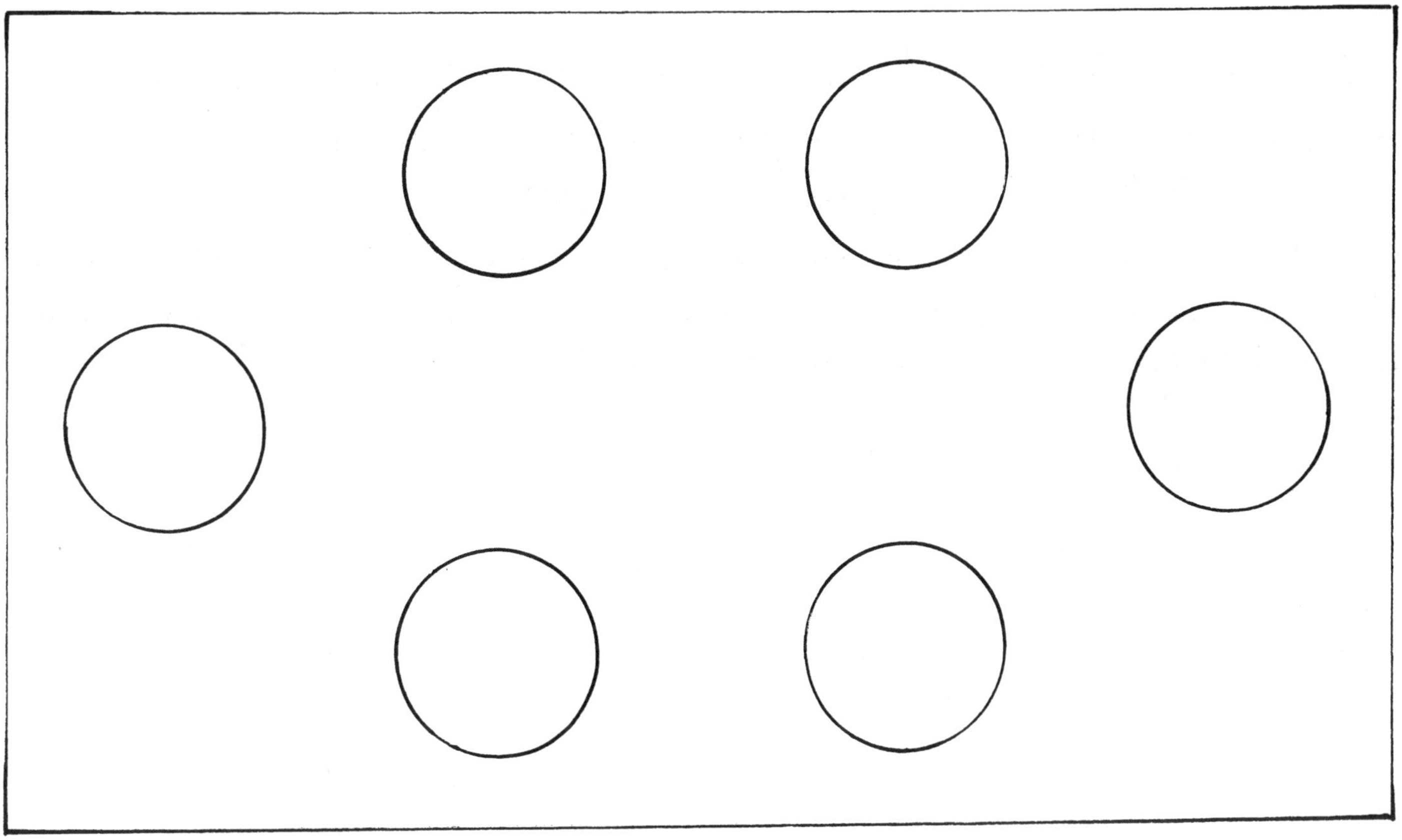

A.

B.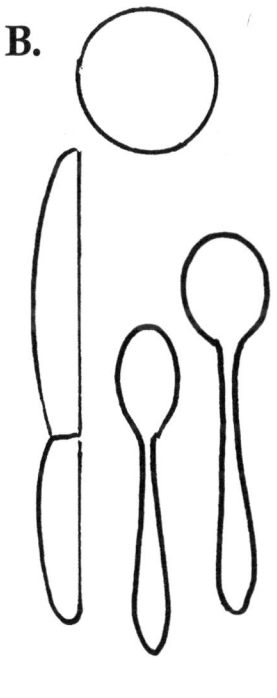

There is always much to do around the house. Like Annie, when guests are coming you can be a big help! Do you know how to set the **dinner table for guests**? To set a table properly, the silverware to be used *first* will be on the *outside*. For example, your salad fork will be to the left of your dinner fork (A), the soup spoon is to the right of the teaspoon and the knife blade faces in towards the plate as shown (B). The glass goes above the knife. You can either place the napkin in the center of the plate or to the left of the fork, having the fold facing inward.

Assignment: Place the dinner settings on the table (above) to the sides of each dinner plate. Give each setting silverware, a napkin and a water glass. You may want to place a vase of colorful flowers as a centerpiece on the table and color it in. This is the way you draw a glass when you are looking down at it.

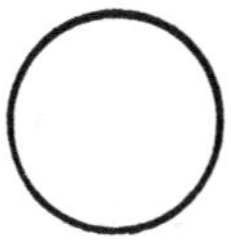

"A cheerful heart is good medicine." Proverbs 17:22

A. Soup Spoon   B. Ladle   C. Serving Spoon

Assignment: Draw your reflection in a soup spoon, a ladle and a serving spoon as shown above. Make funny faces and have fun with this assignment.

Abraham said, "Let me get you something to eat, so you can be refreshed……"   Genesis 18:5

Here are four other things you can do when helping Annie entertain guests.

#1 Ask for their hats.

#3 Invite them in to be seated.

#2 Ask for their coats.

#4 Ask if they would like something to drink.

Assignment: Draw and color a hat in #1, a coat in #2, a chair in #3 and some glasses of water on a tray in #4.

"Do unto others as you would have them do to you." Luke 6:31

Place Annie Here

Can you serve hors d'oeuvres? Many times when Annie's family is having guests over for dinner she will assist in serving snacks.

Assignment: Can you draw Annie in the center of the room with an hors d'oeuvres tray in her hands? Turn to page 9 if you have any problems drawing Annie.

Hors d'oeuvres: A light food served before dinner.

"Teach me knowledge and good judgement." Psalm 119:66

Good Manners Means *NOT* Eating With Your Fingers.

Please, do not eat with your fingers! Always use your silverware. However, there are certain foods that you can eat with your fingers. Do you know what they are? Check the lists below for the seven foods that you may eat with your fingers.

Yes No
- ☐ ☐ 1. Hamburger
- ☐ ☐ 2. Cheese & Crackers
- ☐ ☐ 3. Salad
- ☐ ☐ 4. Pizza
- ☐ ☐ 5. Fried Chicken
- ☐ ☐ 6. Pork Chops
- ☐ ☐ 7. BBQ Ribs
- ☐ ☐ 8. Fried Fish
- ☐ ☐ 9. Chop Sirloin
- ☐ ☐ 10. Prime Rib

Yes No
- ☐ ☐ 11. Steak
- ☐ ☐ 12. Spaghetti
- ☐ ☐ 13. Hot Dog
- ☐ ☐ 14. Meat Loaf
- ☐ ☐ 15. Chicken Chow Mein
- ☐ ☐ 16. Cake
- ☐ ☐ 17. Macaroni & Cheese
- ☐ ☐ 18. Roast Lamb
- ☐ ☐ 19. Lasagna
- ☐ ☐ 20. Pie a la Mode

Assignment: Draw and color the seven foods you can eat with your fingers in the geometric shapes (above). Neatly print the name of the food underneath each drawing.

"Blessed are those who are invited to the wedding supper of the Lamb!" **Revelations 19:9**

More Rules of Dinner Etiquette:
1. Wash your face and hands before dinner.
2. Wait for the adults to be seated at the table before you sit down.
3. When you are seated, remove your napkin from the table and place it on your lap.
4. Wait to begin eating until your guests or parents have begun to do so. Are you going to say grace?
5. Pass the food first to guests or parents before helping yourself.

A. Draw the other Dinner Guest to Annie's

B. What's For Dinner?

C. What's For Dessert?

Assignment: Draw a dinner guest on the other side of Annie in A. Then, place some detail and design in all their clothing. Can you draw and color what's for dinner in B and dessert in C?

"......be ready to do whatever is good." Titus 3:1

More Rules About Dinner Etiquette:
1. Don't reach across someone but ask, "Would you please pass the _____?"
2. Never drink out of a bowl. Use your soup spoon.
3. Please do not slurp your soup or chew with your mouth open.
4. It is rude to make a lot of noise around company.
5. You should answer when spoken to.
6. Do not interrupt when another person is speaking.

A.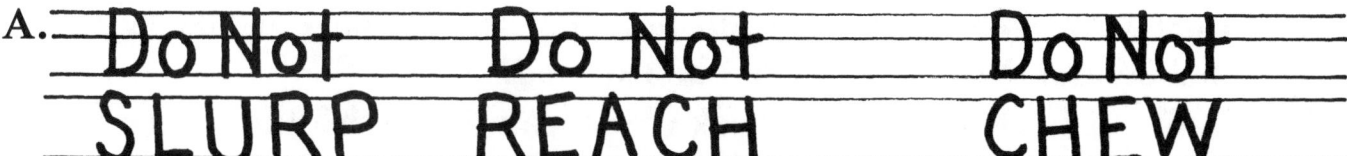

Make guidelines for your letters in A. Have guidelines for both your capital letters and lower case (small) letters.

B.   C.   D.

Assignment: Let's do some lettering. In the figure boxes above write three golden rules about eating: *"Do Not Reach"* in B, *"Do Not Slurp"* in C, and *"Do Not Chew With Your Mouth Open"* in D. Color some nice designs around each golden rule such as flowers and birds.

"Let nothing be wasted." John 6:12

During the Meal.......

1. Proper etiquette calls for you to sit patiently during the entire dinner. Do not squirm in your seat or be fidgety.
2. Be complimentary about the dinner being served to you. It is bad manners to shrug, push away your plate or saying something like, "Ugh, I don't like this stuff!"
3. If possible, eat everything on your plate. God does not want us to be wasteful. He wants us to be "prudent."
4. When you have finished your dinner, place your knife and fork across your plate as in A. Wait patiently until everyone else is finished and then ask, "May I be excused?"
5. Finally, it is always good to ask if you can help with the dishes and with cleaning up.

Remember, God does not want us to be wasteful. Do you remember the story of when Jesus fed the 5,000 people with only a few loaves of bread and several fish? His disciples gathered the scraps, so nothing was wasted. We should not be wasteful with anything; the water we use, the money we spend, or the food we eat.

A. Leave your fork and knife like so when finished.

B. Draw several fish and loaves bread below.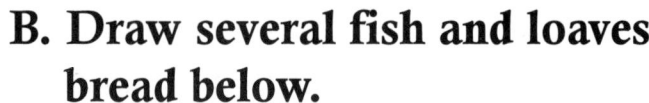

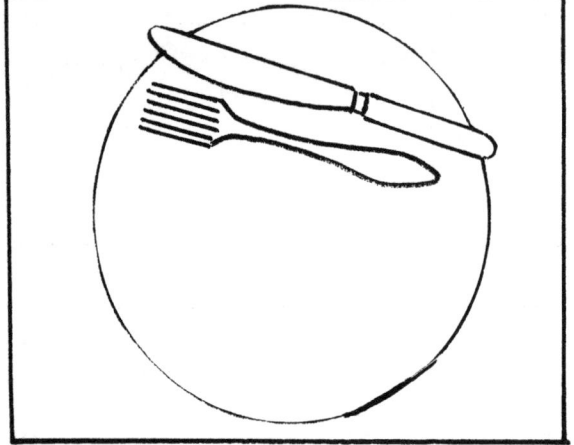

Assignment: Can you draw some fish and a loaf of bread in B?

Prudent: Wise in the management of practical affairs.

"Always be joyful." I Thessalonians 5:16

The Story of Martha and Mary

The story of Martha and Mary is a very interesting one concerning entertaining guests. Do you know who their guest was? It was Jesus. What do you think the two women did? Let's read the story in Luke 10:38-41 and see what happened.

"As Jesus and His disciples were on their way to Jerusalem they came to a village where Martha welcomed them into her home.

Martha became very busy making a big dinner, while Mary sat at Jesus' feet and listened to His teaching.

Martha was working so hard she finally said to Jesus, "Doesn't it seem unfair! I am doing all the work and my sister just sits here. Tell her to help me.

But Jesus said, "Martha, Martha, you are upset over all these details. There is really only one thing needed, and Mary has chosen that good part........"

....

Assignment: Both Martha and Mary were correct in their hospitality to their visitor. However, one of them was more correct. Do you know which woman was more correct? Write on the lines below who was more correct and tell why.

_____
_____
_____
_____
_____
_____
_____
_____

"What is desired in a man is kindness...." Proverbs 19:22

Golden Rules
to Remember

1. Thou shalt love thy neighbor as thyself.
2. Be kind and courteous to all people.
3. Always say "Please" and "Thank you."
4. Make new friends and keep the old.
5. A friend in need is a friend indeed.
6. Be humble and think of others first.
7. Be thankful for all things.
8. God loves a quiet and gentle spirit.
9. Give sincere compliments to others.
10. Words fitly spoken are like apples of gold.
11. Thou shalt not envy.
12. Do not procrastinate.
13. Practice hospitality.
14. Keep a neat and tidy appearance.
15. Practice proper table manners.

The Goops

*"The goops they lick their fingers.
The goops they lick their knives.
They spill their broth on the tablecloth.
Oh, they lead such disgusting lives.
The goops they talk while eating
and loud and fast they chew.
And that is why I'm glad that I
am not a goop, are you?"* — Jack B. Long

"Honor your father and your mother." Exodus 20:12

"And if a house be divided against itself that house cannot stand."

Mark 3:25

A happy home is where everyone is polite and considerate of others. Sometimes it is more difficult to be pleasant at home because we are so familiar with other family members. However, we should behave as well inside our home as do outside. Let's practice being polite and considerate to everyone, especially our family!

If we are not as well-behaved on the inside as we pretend to be on the outside, then we are putting on a false face. Practicing good manners at home will give us the same face all the time!

"But all those who come and listen and obey me are like a man who builds a house on a strong foundation..." Luke 6:48

Drawing a House. Can you draw a house in A? See if you can copy the house below.

A.

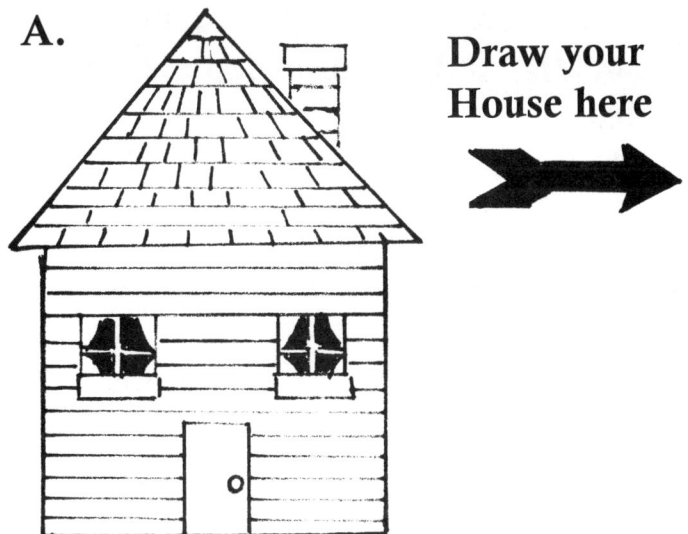

Draw your House here

"Depth" can be added to your drawings by using **"perspective."** See if you can copy the house below using *perspective*.

B.

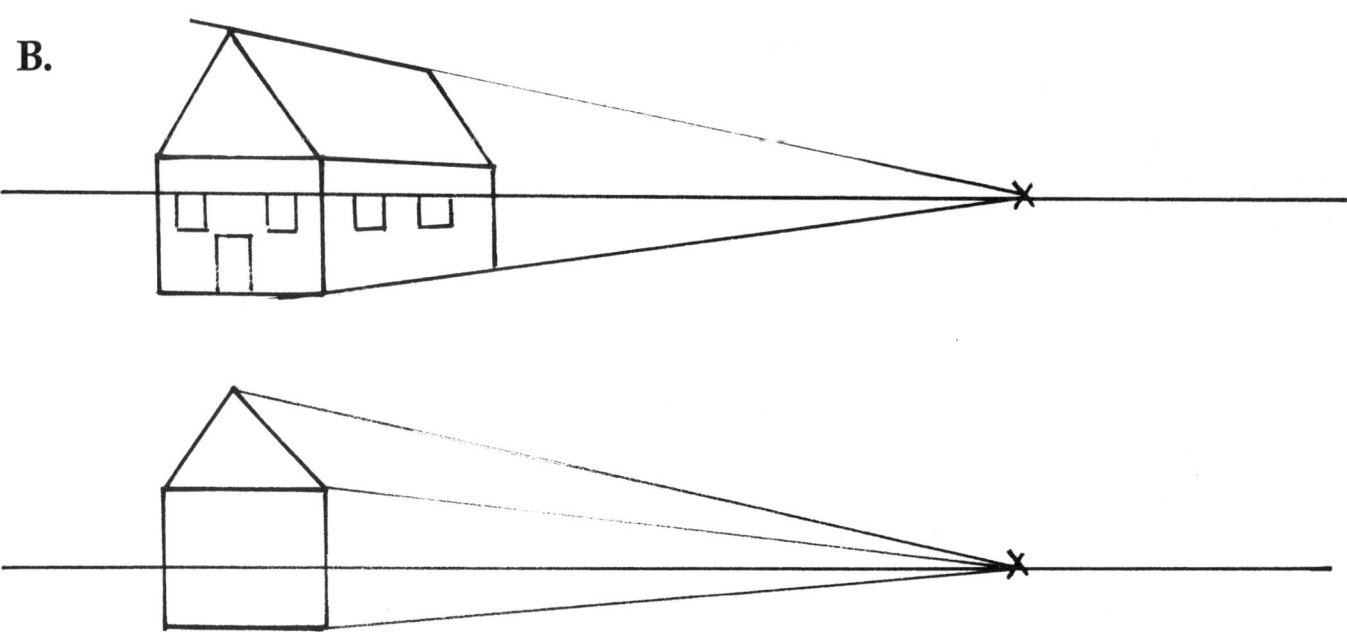

Draw Your House Here

Assignment: Draw the house above in A. Then, draw the second house in B using *"perspective."* Use a ruler for these drawings to keep your lines straight.

51

"....live in peace and quietness, spending our time in godly living and thinking much about the Lord."   I Timothy 2:2

Watching Television

As Annie grows, she spends very little time watching television. Although there are some good educational programs, television teaches very little about being well-mannered and refined. Instead, Annie spends her spare time developing her talents and hobbies.

Things I Like to Do

1. _____

2. _____

3. _____

4. _____

A.

B.

Assignment: Can you name four things that you like to do more than watch television? It could be picking flowers, riding a bicycle, playing with your pets, flying a kite, doing artwork, or anything else you like. Draw a picture of two of those things in the figure boxes (A & B). This evening, do two of these things without watching any television and see how much fun you can have!

"He who values grace and truth is the king's friend."

Proverbs 22:11

Refinement

"Refinement" is a wonderful quality that grown-ups love for children to have. For instance, do you know who Mozart is? Beethoven? Handel? Chopin? They are famous classical composers of music. What about Rembrandt? Van Gogh? Michelangelo? Peter Paul Reubens? Claude Monet? They are all famous masters of painting. Our parents would like to see us grow up with all of the social graces, and this includes using proper words, being pleasant, having good manners, and being *"refined."*

Assignment: Go to the library and look up two artists, Vincent van Gogh and Claude Monet. Take the books home and copy one of their paintings on a plain sheet of white paper. Do this while listening to Mozart, Beethoven, Handel or Chopin. You can find classical music in the library if you haven't any at home. Do you find the music inspiring? Finally, during dinner, discuss the piece of artwork you did and the classical music you listened to with your parents.

Refinement: Elegance of manner; politeness.

"Say only what is good and helpful to those you are talking to, and what will give them a blessing."   Ephesians 4:29

Answering the Telephone

Answer the telephone with a cheery "Hello!" If you really want to be proper you might say,

"*Good morning, this is the* _____ *residence.*"

The proper response from the person calling might be, "*Hello, this is Mrs. Smith. Is your mother at home?*"
Then you might reply, "*Yes she is, one moment please.*"

******** Do not slam the phone down ******
*** Do not yell for your mother to come to the phone, but
politely tell her that someone is on the phone ***

When Annie calls, she greets the person and let's them know who is calling. "Good evening, this is Annie. Is Beth in?" The proper response by Beth would be, "This is she." Beth does not say, "This is her," or "This is me."   A.   B.

Assignment: Let's pretend you have just called Annie. Do you remember what to say when someone answers the phone? Write your greeting in the bubble above the figure in A. What will Annie's response be? Can you draw the bubble above her head, and the guidelines with her response in B?

"Every man's life is a fairy-tale written by God's fingers."
Hans Christian Anderson

Writing a Formal Letter

There will be many times in your life when you will be called to write a formal letter. A formal letter is a letter that is written properly, using good penmanship, grammar and spelling. However, a formal letter does not have to be fancy. Just write it the very best you can. You can write a formal letter to your congressman, senator, or even the president of the United States. It doesn't matter how old you are or who you are. As citizens, we all have the right to voice our feelings. Have you ever written a formal letter to someone important?

Practice Good Penmanship

Aa Bb Cc Dd Ed Ff Gg Hh Ii

Jj Kk Ll Mm Nn Oo Pp Qq Rr

Ss Tt Uu Vv Ww Xx Yy Zz

Assignment: Write a formal letter to a politician. It may be your congressman, senator or even the local mayor. Let him know how you feel about something. Or you may simply want to compliment him on the good job he is doing. Practice your **penmanship** above by copying the alphabet in your very best handwriting. You may want to use a nice pen for this. Then, when you are finished, write someone who represents you in government using nice stationary and fine penmanship.

Penmanship: Quality of writing.

"You are the fairest of all; your words are filled with grace."
Psalm 45:2

Speaking with the Proper Pronunciation

"Lazy" language is when we slur our words. Do you speak clearly and pronounce each syllable (sil-a-bul) in a word? Proper pronunciation takes training and effort. Try reading stories out loud and pronouncing each syllable slowly and precisely.

Today's exercise is to say the two verses below five times each without slipping. These are called *"tongue twisters."* They are fun to do and help in teaching us how to speak with proper pronunciation. Look at the statements, and then without looking, recite each five times. Pronounce every syllable slowly and precisely.

Tongue Twister #1: *"She sells sea shells by the seashore."*

Tongue Twister #2: *"Black bug's blood."*

Assignment: Draw and color a sunset on the water with an island and palm trees in the frame above. Then, draw and color sea shells in the frame.

"So God created man in His own image." — Genesis 1:27

Having Good Posture

"Sit up, please." Do your parents ever say that to you? They remind you to do this so you will keep your back straight and develop good posture. Annie always sits up straight. She even practices walking with a book on her head which keeps her body perfectly upright.

A. Good Posture

B. Poor Posture

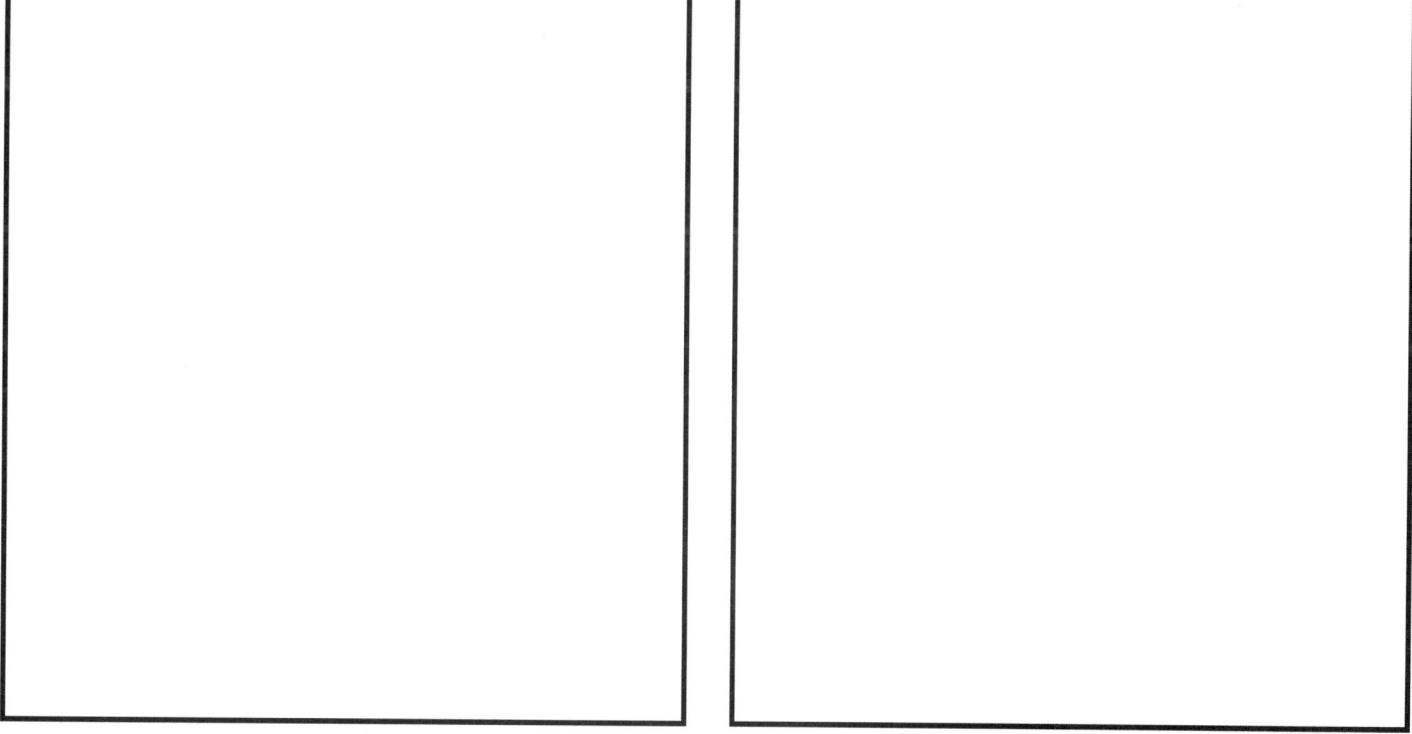

Assignment: Take a book and place it on your head. Then, see if you can walk around the house for five minutes without dropping it. You should do this often to create good posture. Also, draw someone with good posture in A and poor posture in B.

"Children, obey your parents in everything, for this pleases the Lord."
				Colossians 3:20

Obeying Your Parents

Obeying your parents is not something you might do if you feel like it, but something you are commanded to do by God. Why does He tells you to obey our parents? Because they know what is right and wrong for you. Because they work very hard during the day and need your help. Because you are to respect those who have authority over you.

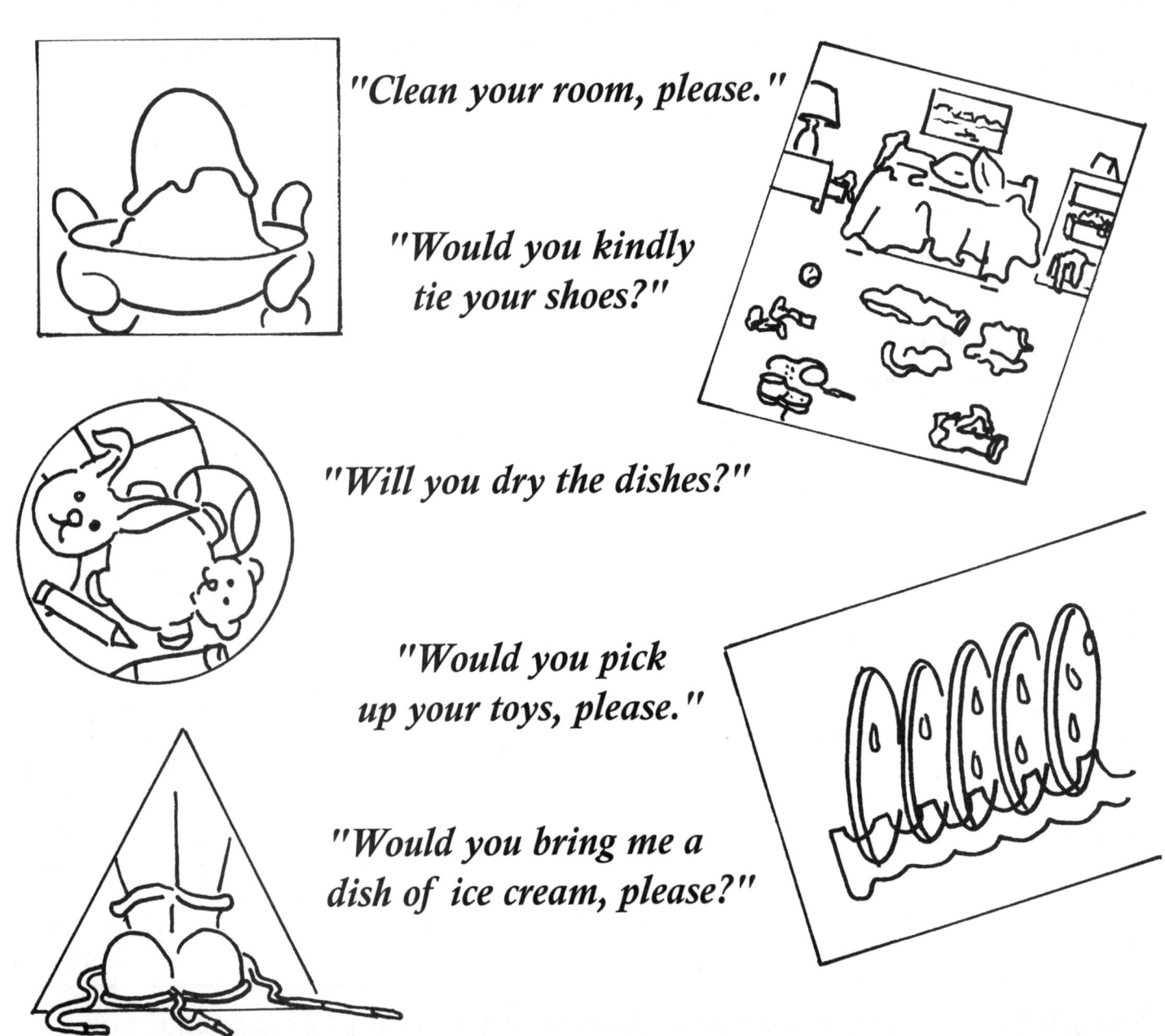

"Clean your room, please."

"Would you kindly tie your shoes?"

"Will you dry the dishes?"

"Would you pick up your toys, please."

"Would you bring me a dish of ice cream, please?"

Assignment: Connect the drawings with a pencil line to the commands given from your parents and color each picture with your colored pencils.

"Do everything without complaining or arguing so that you may become blameless and pure, children of God without fault...."

Philippians 2:14-15

Running Errands

Have you ever stood back and watched your father or mother working? Who does the dishes? Who washes the car? Who washes the clothes? Who cuts the grass? Your parents work very, very hard. And they need your help. Children should run errands for their parents. This is a way of helping when they are busy and also teaches children responsibility. So, whenever your father or mother asks you to run an errand for them, do it with great joy knowing that you being are a big help!

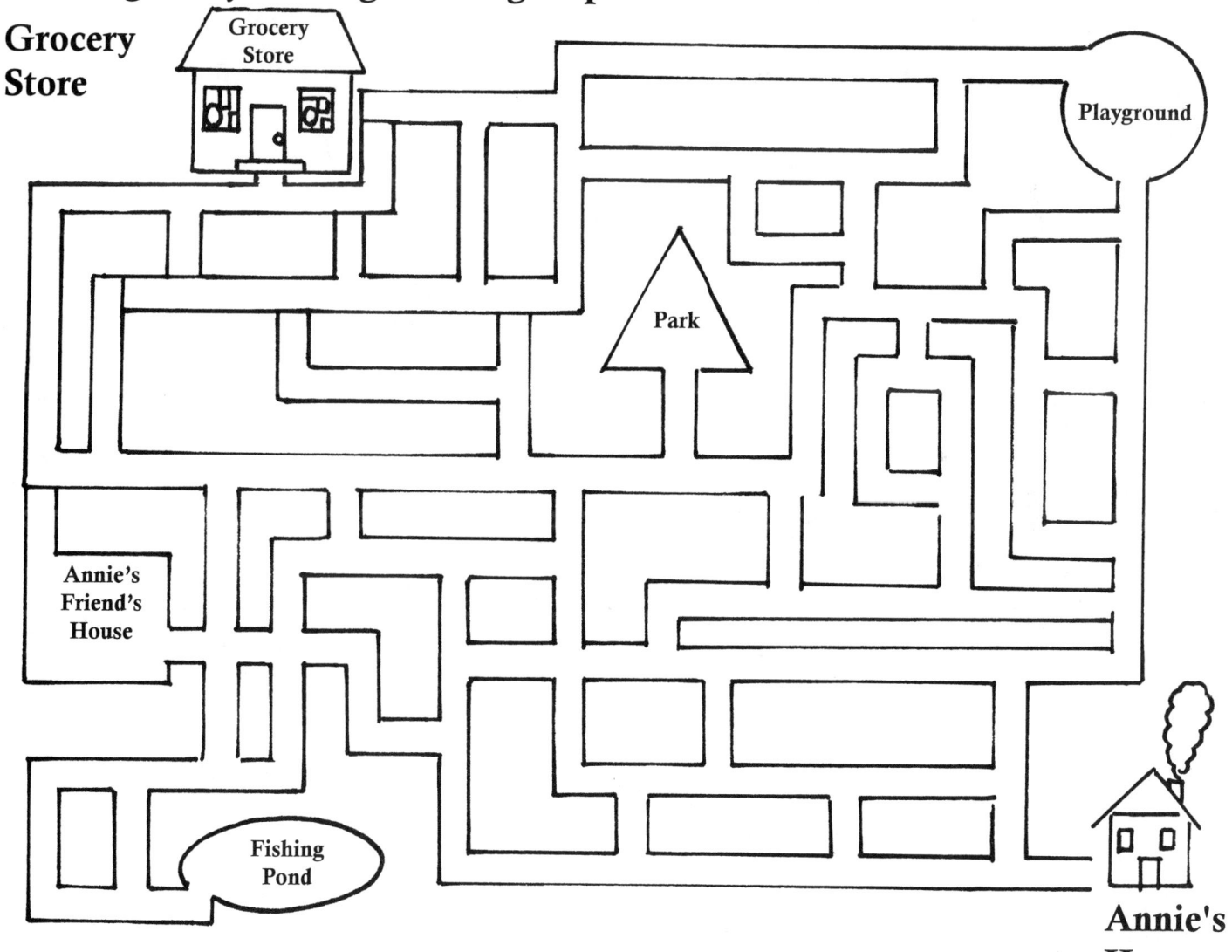

Assignment: Annie must go to the grocery store for her mother. Can you take her through the maze and bring her to the store as soon as possible? Remember, she mustn't stop at the playground or her friend's house or the local fish pond, but must go directly to the store and then return home.

"Nothing in all creation is hidden from God's sight."

Hebrews 4:13

Putting All Your Ducks In A Row

Do you know what *putting all your ducks in a row* means? It means to have everything organized and in order. You can do this each day by making a list and doing everything that has to be done. Cleaning your room, folding your clothes, putting your shoes away, picking up your toys and so forth. This not only puts *all your ducks in a row,* but also makes your parents very happy!

A. Things I Need To Do: B.

#1. _____

#2. _____

#3. _____

#4. _____

#5. _____

#6. _____

#7. _____

#8. _____

#9. _____

Assignment: In A, make a list of the things you need to do each morning. In B, draw some of the things you need to do in the geometric shapes.

Jesus said, "....*I tell you the truth, when you were younger you dressed yourself."*
John 21:18

Let's Get Dressed

One of the responsibilities we should learn as a child is to dress ourselves. We should put on clean clothes, tuck in our shirts and blouses, tie our shoes, brush our teeth, and comb our hair. Having a nice appearance is our own responsibility and a good appearance makes a good impression on others!

Assignment: Can you put clothes and shoes on the boys and girls above? Turn to page 93 and color the clothes. Then, cut out some of the clothes and paste them on the children. Can you make some more cutouts?

Picture A

Assignment: Can you help Annie straighten up the house for her mother? There are 10 things that are out of order in Picture A compared to Picture B. Do you know what they are? See if you can find them.

Picture B

"And the Child grew and became strong; He was filled with wisdom and the grace of God was upon Him." Luke 2:40

".....whatever is right.....whatever is lovely.....think about such things."
                                                    Philippians 4:8

Going Shopping

Have you ever seen children who go shopping with their mother and *throw tantrums* right in front of everyone? They lay on the floor, bang their feet, scream and cry until they get their way. This is really an embarrassment to everyone. However, when Annie goes shopping with her mother she is peaceful and quiet, not demanding anything. She is patient with her mother's chores and finds little things to do to occupy her time. And do you know what? Her mother is so pleased with her behavior that Annie receives a better reward than any of the children who whine and pout to get their way.

Assignment: Can you draw an ice cream in Annie's hand and place some balloons in her other hand? Color in your picture when finished.

"If you fully obey all of these commandments...the Lord will bless you with good crops and healthy cattle, and prosper everything you do......"

Deuteronomy 28:1,8

Purchasing Groceries

Annie does such a good job shopping with her mother that her mother lets her do some of the shopping. Can you assist Annie? Her mother has given her $10.00 to go to Mr. Jacobson's Market. Her mother wants her to buy a quart of milk for $1.50, a loaf of bread for $2.00, a dozen eggs for $2.00, and 3 apples for $1.00. Would you assist Annie at the counter? How much change should she receive after paying for the groceries?

A Glass of Milk

A Loaf of Bread

A Basket of Eggs

3 Apples

Assignment: After you have figured out how much money Annie has left, draw a glass of milk, a loaf of bread, a basket of eggs and 3 apples in the figure boxes above. Can you letter the name and cost of each item using guidelines. For example: 3 apples $1.00

"....for God loves a cheerful giver." **II Corinthians 9:7**

Birthdays & Anniversaries

Happy Birthday! Do you remember the dates of your parents' birthdays? Do you know their anniversary? Annie becomes more excited about their birthdays then she does her own! She likes to plan ahead by saving money for their presents and by making them special birthday cards. You should always remember the special birthday and anniversary dates for your family and friends. Your thoughtfulness will really make someone happy!

Assignment: Can you design a birthday card? Turn to page 94 and design a birthday card for someone special. Be creative and colorful! You can also make an envelope (see page 89).

"You saw me before I was born...."   Psalm 139:16

Happy Birthday!

Assignment: Can you help Annie prepare for a birthday party? First, letter *Happy Birthday* on the banner above. Make sure to use the guidelines to keep your letters straight. Decorate the room with party favors! Draw and color some balloons above the table. Can you draw some gifts and toys on the table?

"Blessed are the pure at heart, for they shall see God."

Matthew 5:8

Going to Church

Do you like going to church? Some children do not put on their best behavior when they go to church on Sunday mornings. They squirm in their seats, talk and disturb the people around them.

Every Sunday morning Annie becomes very excited about going to church. Do you know why? Because she feels God in her heart and can almost see Him. She loves Jesus and learns so much about Him. Church should be a very exciting time, knowing that it is a place to praise God and to listen for His voice.

Assignment: Can you draw a church on a hill in the picture frame above? Draw some trees in the background and people coming to church as illustrated. You may want to start your drawing off lightly with your yellow colored pencil and then go over it with your black pen. See how much detail you can put in your picture and then color with your colored pencils.

"Do things in such a way that everyone can see you are honest clear through."
Romans 12:17

Honesty is the Best Policy

"*Integrity*" means honesty. Sometimes telling the truth actually hurts. There will be times when something has happened and it would seem easier for you not to tell the truth. However, if you continually tell the truth, being completely honest, everyone will like and respect you much, much more. They will learn to trust you and what you say.

A. Take a long strip of paper and fold it back and forth.

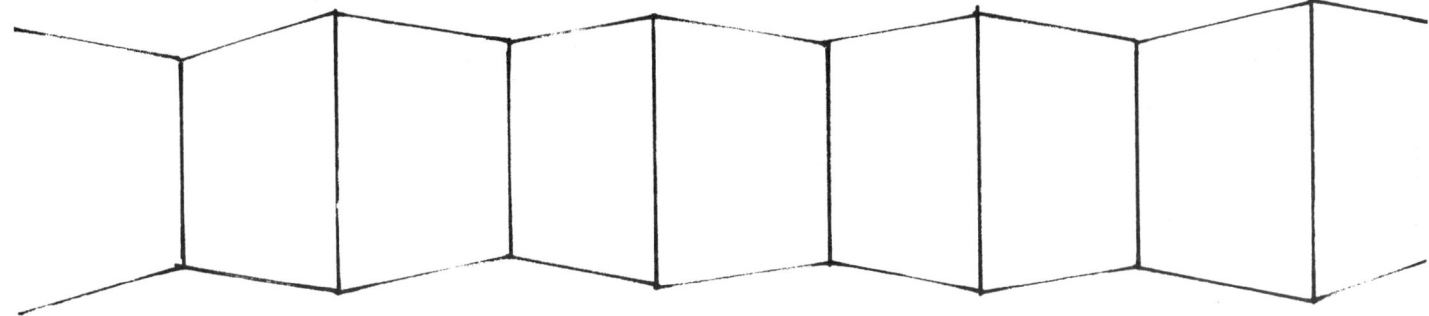

B. Draw a design on the front making sure the edges of the drawing touch the sides.

C. Cut out the design making sure you don't cut the edges that touch the sides.

D. Open it up and you have a chain of delightful figures!

Assignment: Do you know how to make a chain of angels? Follow the instructions above and then turn to page 97 and complete the cutout series of angels. When you open it, you will have a chain of angels.

Integrity: Honesty.

"Don't quarrel with anyone. Be at peace with everyone, just as much as possible."
Romans 12:18

Riding in the Car

Riding in a car is a time when we have to be especially considerate of others and on our best behavior. Have you ever seen children who squirm around in the car or jump up and down, or brothers and sisters who fight and argue while their mother or father is driving? How about children who whine and complain saying, "How much further……?" or "I'm bor-e-e-e-d." This can be very annoying and even dangerous. The person driving needs to give his or her undivided attention to the traffic and street signs.

Annie has learned how to occupy her time so that she is never bored or complaining. Whenever she goes on a trip with her parents she takes along a book to read. She even brings some of her paper for drawing or writing letters. But most of all, Annie likes to write in her journal each and every day. She writes about the weather and what she is doing and where she has been. She also puts drawings in her journal to show some of the things that were around her that day. But remember, the most important thing is that Annie is never bored.

My Journal

_____

_____

_____

_____

_____

_____

_____

Assignment: Can you write about your day on the lines above? Don't forget to draw some things that remind you of your day.

"Let your light so shine before men that they may see your good deeds and honor your Father who is in heaven."   Matthew 5:16

Going Out to Dinner

Do you ever go out to dinner with your parents? That is when you should be on your very best behavior. Going out to dinner is a special time when people like to act the most sophisticated. No matter where we are or who we are with, if we work on our manners and etiquette at all times, we will add a certain element of grace to our personalities. People are naturally attracted to children who are polite, considerate and friendly, so let's work on our manners at all times.

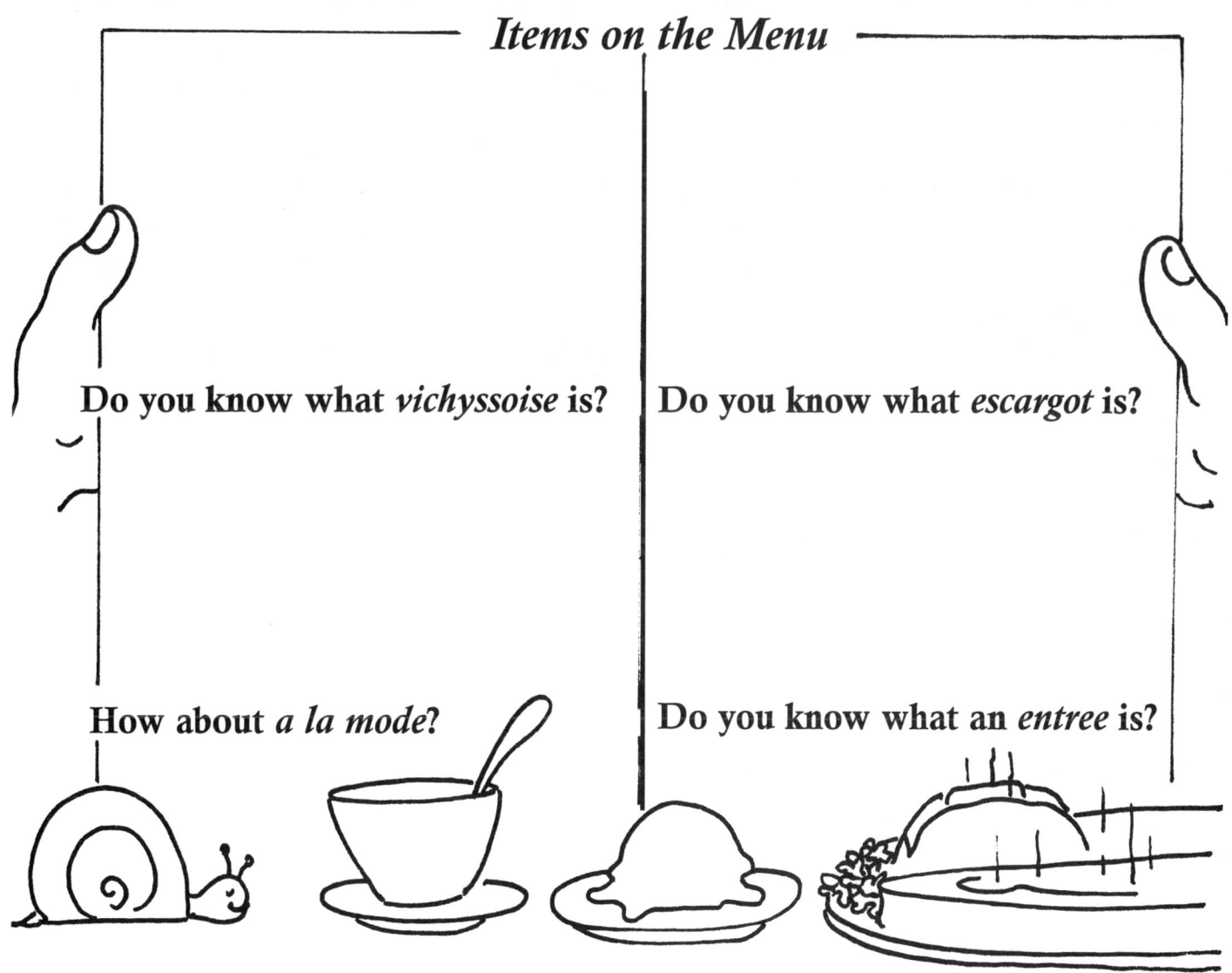

Items on the Menu

Do you know what *vichyssoise* is?

Do you know what *escargot* is?

How about *a la mode*?

Do you know what an *entree* is?

Assignment: Take the four items above and draw them in the proper square. If you do not know what the word means, use your dictionary.

Sophisticated: Having a refined nature.

"Lie quietly upon your bed in silent meditation."   Psalm 4:4

The Story of Young Samuel

.....Meanwhile little Samuel was helping the Lord by assisting Eli, an old priest. Messages from the Lord were very rare in those days, but one night after Eli had gone to bed, and Samuel was sleeping in the temple, the Lord called out, "Samuel! Samuel!"

"Yes," Samuel replied, "What is it?" He jumped up and ran to Eli. "Here I am. What do you want?" he asked.

"I didn't call you," Eli said, "Go on back to bed." So he did. Then the Lord called again, "Samuel!" And again Samuel jumped up and ran to Eli.

"Yes," he asked, "What do you need?" " I didn't call you, my son," Eli said, "Go on back to bed."

Young Samuel had never had a message from God before. So now the Lord called the third time, and once more Samuel jumped up and ran to Eli.

"Yes," he asked, "What do you need?" Then Eli realized it was the Lord who had spoken to the child. So he said to Samuel, "Go and lie down and if He calls again, say 'Yes, Lord, I'm listening.'" So Samuel went back to bed.

And the Lord came and called as before, "Samuel! Samuel!"

And Samuel replied, "Yes, Lord, I am listening."   I Samuel 3:1-10

Assignment: Can you draw a picture of young Samuel in the frame above? Use your colored pencils.

Elders

With the aged is wisdom; and with length of days comes understanding"
Job 12:12

"I have been young and now I am old." Psalm 37:25

Grandmom & Grandpop

Annie loves to visit her grandmom and grandpop and they are always happy to see their little granddaughter. Annie thinks that elderly people are a lot like children because they like to have fun doing the same type of things. However, elderly people like your grandparents move much slower than children because their bodies are not as flexible. So Annie is always gentle and mild mannered around her grandparents, just like when she plays with her kittens. Her grandparents like peace and quiet and Annie is careful to be of a gentle and quiet spirit when she visits. Most of all, Annie likes to bring her grandparents a present! What she especially loves to give them is her artwork. It really makes them happy. And you know what? They hang her pictures in their favorite art gallery, the kitchen. Every time Annie brings a piece of art to their home, her grandmother attaches it to the big door of their refrigerator with a kitchen magnet.

A "POP-UP" FOR POP-POP

Make a foldout shape like the angels on page 97. Using a glue stick or paste, glue the back of the first angel on the left side of your card and the back of the last angel to the right side. Color around your pop-up. Place a greeting on it. Fold it closed. Open it. And pop! Out they come!

Assignment: Turn to page 97-99 and do a pop-up card. You may want to use your angels for this. You can write a colorful greeting on the card.

"Commit everything you do to the Lord. Trust Him to help you and He will." Psalm 37:5

Sending a Photo Card

"All purpose" cards are cards that we can use for any occasions, or you can send to a friend just to say *"hello."*

One of Annie's favorite cards to make is a photograph card. They are great to use for any occasion.

Materials:

- card (turn to page 101)
- photographs or pictures
- scissors
- glue stick
- ruler
- pen

Directions:

1. Ask your parents for copies of photographs of your family, your dog, cat, flowers, animals at the zoo or anything else you like. If you don't have any photographs to use, cut pictures out of magazines.

2. Cut out a card like the one on page 101 and fold it in two.

3. Lightly apply a glue stick to the back of your photos or pictures and adhere the pictures to the front of your card.

4. Annie likes to write a favorite scripture verse on the inside of her card, and sometimes decorates the card with little designs.

5. Finally, make your own envelope and mail your card!

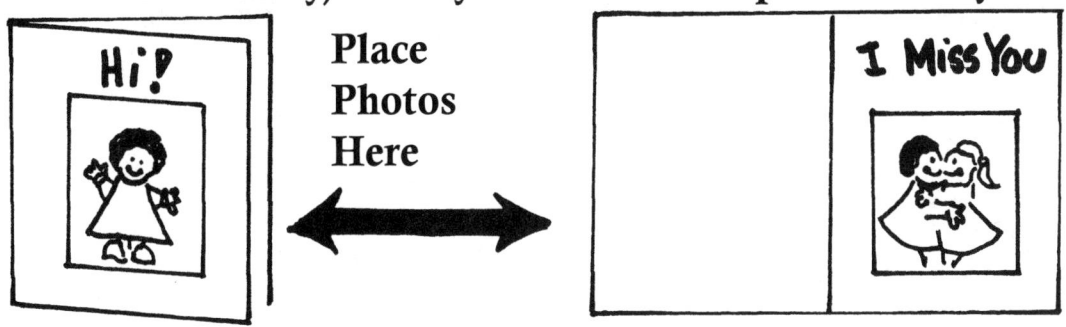

Assignment: Follow the directions above to make a photo card on page 101, and make an envelope on page 89.

Jesus said, ".....I tell you the truth, when you were younger you dressed yourself....but when you are old you will stretch out your hands and someone else will dress you." John 21:18

Visiting a Nursing Home

No one enjoys visits from children more than elderly people. It is an excellent time for children to put on their best behavior, to use proper etiquette, and be a wonderful blessing to them. A visit to the nursing home is a wonderful treat for elderly people. Whenever Annie visits the local nursing home she is always respectful to her elders, saying "Yes sir" or "No ma'am."

Remember the dried flowers we stored in-between the pages of a big book? Let's take them out now and make a card like the one on page 103 to take to the nursing home.

Pressed Flower Cards

Pressed flowers, leaves, ferns and grasses can be made into lovely cards for every occasion. Remember: the flowers should be collected and dried well before you need them.

Materials:
    1. Delicate flowers, leaves and ferns (bulky flowers do not press well)
    2. Magazines or books
    3. Tweezers
    4. Elmer's glue
    5. Card paper

Assignment: Let's make a pressed flower card. Follow the directions below and turn to page 103.

    1. To press flowers, leaves, etc., spread them flat between pages of old magazines or a catalog for **at least 2 weeks**. The colors may fade, but that is part of their charm.

    2. Remove delicate flowers with tweezers and pleasantly arrange them on your card before gluing.

    3. Take a tiny dab of Elmer's glue on a Q-tip and brush onto the back of dried flowers. Make sure the flowers are well glued and be careful the glue does not show. Let the glue dry.

    4. Add a greeting to your card and make an envelope (page 89).

"Let each of you look out not only for his own interests, but also for the interests of others."   Philippians 2:4

Offering Your Seat

Have you ever been on a crowded mode of transportation like a bus, train or subway? Were there people standing? Did you notice how unhappy the people were who had to stand, especially elderly people? They have all had a long day and are very tired. If you are seated, sometimes it is a generous gesture for you to offer your seat to an elderly person. You are young, bouncy and strong and it would mean a great deal more for an elderly person to be seated than for you. And, if you do give them your seat, God will give you your reward.

A. Automobile

B. Bus

C. Train

D. Airplane

Assignment: Can you draw an automobile? A bus? A train? An airplane? Draw and color them above.

"We who are strong ought to bear with the failings and the frailties....of the weak." Romans 15:1

Helping Someone Across the Street

Have you ever seen an elderly person trying to cross a street? Did you notice how slow they move? Also, they may seem a little confused by all the traffic and noise. It is good to assist the elderly whenever possible. You could even offer to carry their bags. They will be very thankful!

Assignment: Can you draw yourself helping the elderly lady crossing the street? Your hand helping her's has already been drawn for you. Can you print STOP in the stop sign? Also, see if you can add some details to the rest of your picture. Complete the drawing with your black drawing pen, putting in as much detail as possible.

"I was sick and you visited Me."   Matthew 25:36

Visiting Someone Who is Sick

Sometimes you have to visit elderly people or relatives who are not feeling well. We visit them to cheer them up. One way of cheering them up is to bring them flowers. Another way is to take them one of your handmade cards. Still another way is to write a story and to read it to them. When you read your story, watch and see how much it cheers them up, especially if you have some pictures with it!

Title: _____

_____
_____
_____
_____
_____
_____
_____
_____
_____
_____
_____
_____

Assignment: In the space above, write a story about a cat, some bananas, an umbrella, a bird with a hurt wing or a red balloon. Draw pictures to go along with your story. Quite possible, you could read this to elderly people when they need to be cheered up.

"But when you are old, you will stretch out your hands, and others will direct you."
John 21:18

Being Mindful of Neighbors

We should all be respectful of our neighbors and our neighbors' property, and we should be especially thoughtful around our elderly neighbors. Elderly people have a much more simple and peaceful lifestyle than younger people, so please be mindful of this and considerate of the way they desire to live.

Whenever Annie goes by her elderly neighbors' homes she keeps her voice low so she doesn't disturb them. She never runs across their property or lets her dog go "potty" on their grass. If her parents approve, she asks if there is anything she can do to help them, like bringing in their newspaper or replacing the lids on their trash cans. God wants us to take care of the elderly, especially when they have a difficult time doing some things for themselves.

A.

My Miniature Map

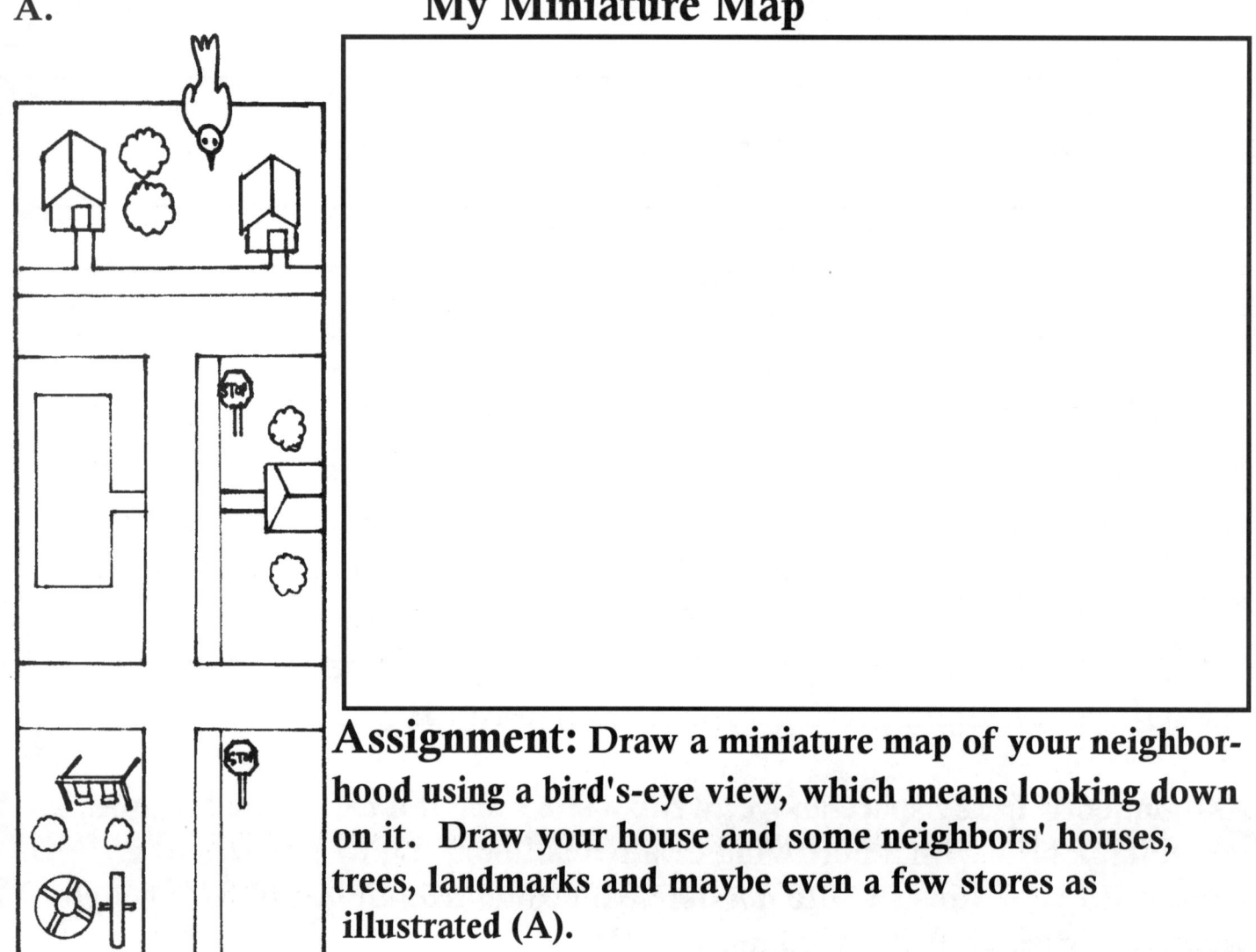

Assignment: Draw a miniature map of your neighborhood using a bird's-eye view, which means looking down on it. Draw your house and some neighbors' houses, trees, landmarks and maybe even a few stores as illustrated (A).

Name:_____ Grade:_____

Date:_____

EXAMINATION

"Study to show thyself approved." 2 Timothy 2:15

Little Annie's School of Etiquette & Good Manners

I. Matching (5 points each). Draw a line from each word to its definition (Answers appear on bottom of page 82).

1. Host
2. Courteous
3. Envy
4. Procrastinate
5. Hospitable
6. Flattery
7. Hors d'oeuvres
8. Compliment
9. Refinement
10. Integrity
11. Prudent
12. Sophisticated

A. Having a refined nature.
B. An admiring remark.
C. Honesty.
D. Being polite and considerate.
E. A light food served before dinner.
F. Elegance of manner.
G. Insincere praise.
H. Wise in the management of practical affairs.
I. To want what belongs to another.
J. To be warm and friendly to guests.
K. A person who receives guests for a social visit.
L. To put off tomorrow what you should do today.

II. True or False (5 pts each). Put a "T" or "F" next to each sentence if you believe it is true or false.

1. You should feed your animals before you sit down to eat.
2. If you have something to say you should interrupt others.
3. Children should start eating before everyone else.
4. Children are supposed to be noisy around adults because grown ups like that type of behavior.
5. It is better to give than receive.

III. Essay (15 pts). Write a short essay in 25 to 50 words explaining why it is important to know etiquette and proper manners when dealing with other people.

Jesus said, "You shall love the Lord your God with all your heart, with all your soul, and with all your mind. This is the first and great commandment. And the second is like it: You shall love your neighbor as yourself."   Matthew 22:37-39

God gives us laws and guidelines to live by. The Book of Proverbs is good for teaching us how to behave. The Lord also gives us the Ten Commandments which are Godly laws to live by. Below are some of the simple rules of good etiquette that you may also want to remember.

Ten Commandments of Good Etiquette

1. Lead a life that is pleasing to God.
2. Obey your father and mother.
3. Always be thankful for everything.
4. Let your words be kind and respectful.
5. Smile.
6. Always have a good appearance.
7. Practice good posture and proper diction.
8. Giving is better than receiving.
9. Be a good listener.
10. Respect your elders.

Assignment: Are there any other rules of etiquette and good manners that you know? Write them below:

11. _____

12. _____

13. _____

14. _____

15. _____

Answers to Examination (page 81)
Part I: 1-K, 2-D, 3-I, 4-L, 5-J, 6-G, 7-E, 8-B, 9-F, 10-C, 11-H, 12-A
Part II: 1-T, 2-F, 3-F, 4-F, 5-T

Cut & Paste

"For it is precept upon precept... rule upon rule... here a little, there a little."
Isaiah 28:10

Stickers

Materials Needed:

1. Colored Markers
2. Scissors
3. Glue Stick

Assignment: On the next page are many designs for you to color, cut out and use on birthday cards, envelopes or other artwork. Color them in and cut them out as you need them. You may want to create some with your own imagination or find some cartoons or illustrations and copy them. Then, when you are ready to use one, simply cut it out and glue it on!

Let's Make Our Own Stickers!

85

Assignment: We are going to make a greeting card for one of our friends! Cut out your card on page 87. Fold it in half making a nice crease by running the side of a ruler down your fold. Color the outside and the inside. Put a message or greeting in it and then send it in the mail! Turn to page 88 to learn how to make an envelope.

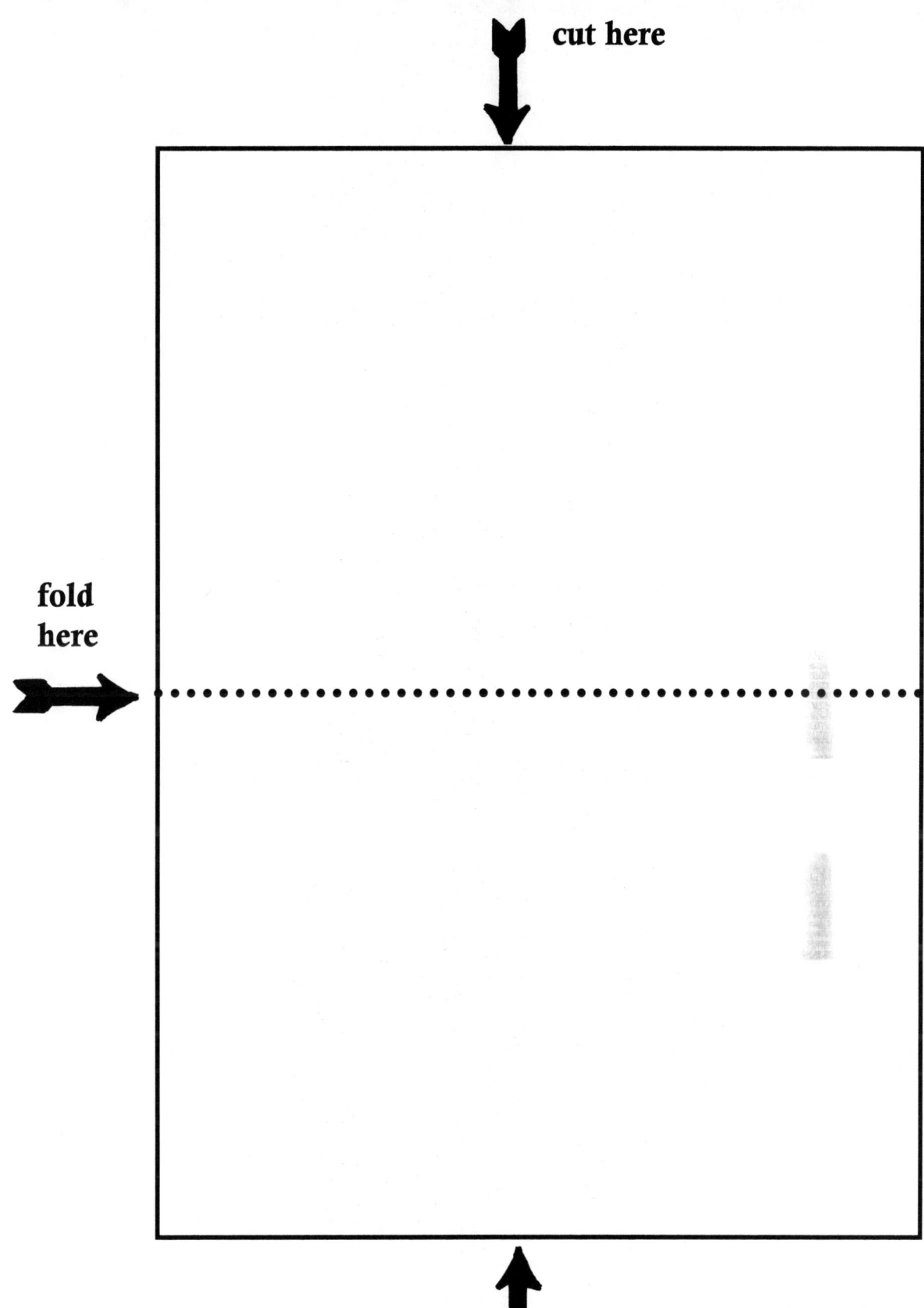

Assignment: We are going to make our card 3 1/2" by 5". Cut out the card above and fold it in half at the dotted line.

Assignment: On page 89 you will find directions for making envelopes. Please do not cut out the illustrations for making envelopes, but use them as a guide. You can use any type of paper you like for an envelope. Colored construction paper will make an especially nice, bright envelope!

Making an Envelope

Here's how to make your own envelope. Plain paper works just fine, or you can use colored paper.

Materials:
Card, paper, scissors, glue stick

E.

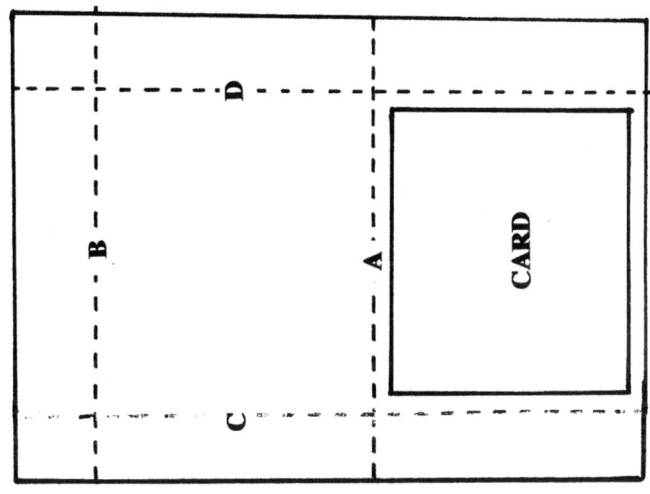

1. Place your card on the envelope paper as in illustration E.

2. Fold the envelope at A to fit the card. Then, fold your paper again at B.
Unfold the paper and then fold the two sides C and D. Remove the card and unfold the envelope.

F.

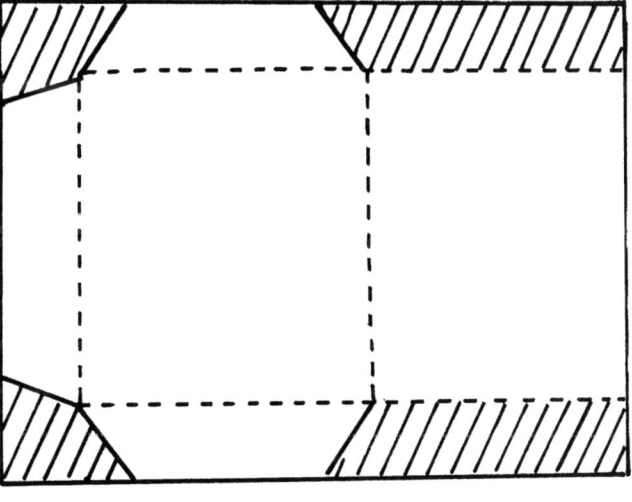

3. Cut out the shaded areas as shown in illustration F. Make a practice envelope first to get the feel of it.

4. Your envelope is ready to glue together as in G. Fold at A. Glue or scotch tape the two side flaps (B) over to make your envelope.

G.

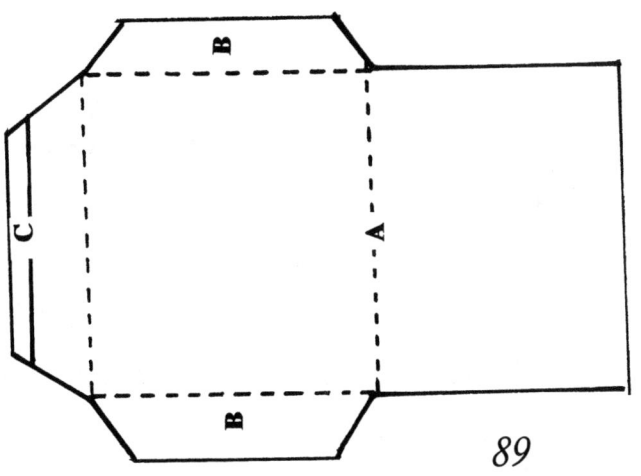

5. When dry, insert card and either glue (C) to seal, or glue a handmade sticker to seal your envelope.

Making a *Thank You* Card

Assignment: Making a *Thank You* card is just like making a greeting card, except we will letter *Thank You* on it in appreciation for what someone has done for us. Cut out the card on the next page. Remember to fold your card in half. Draw and color a nice design on the front. Are you going to use some of your stickers? You may even want to cut out the letters *Thank You* or do the lettering yourself. Save your card and send it to someone when they have done something special for you.

Thank You! *Thank You!*

cut here

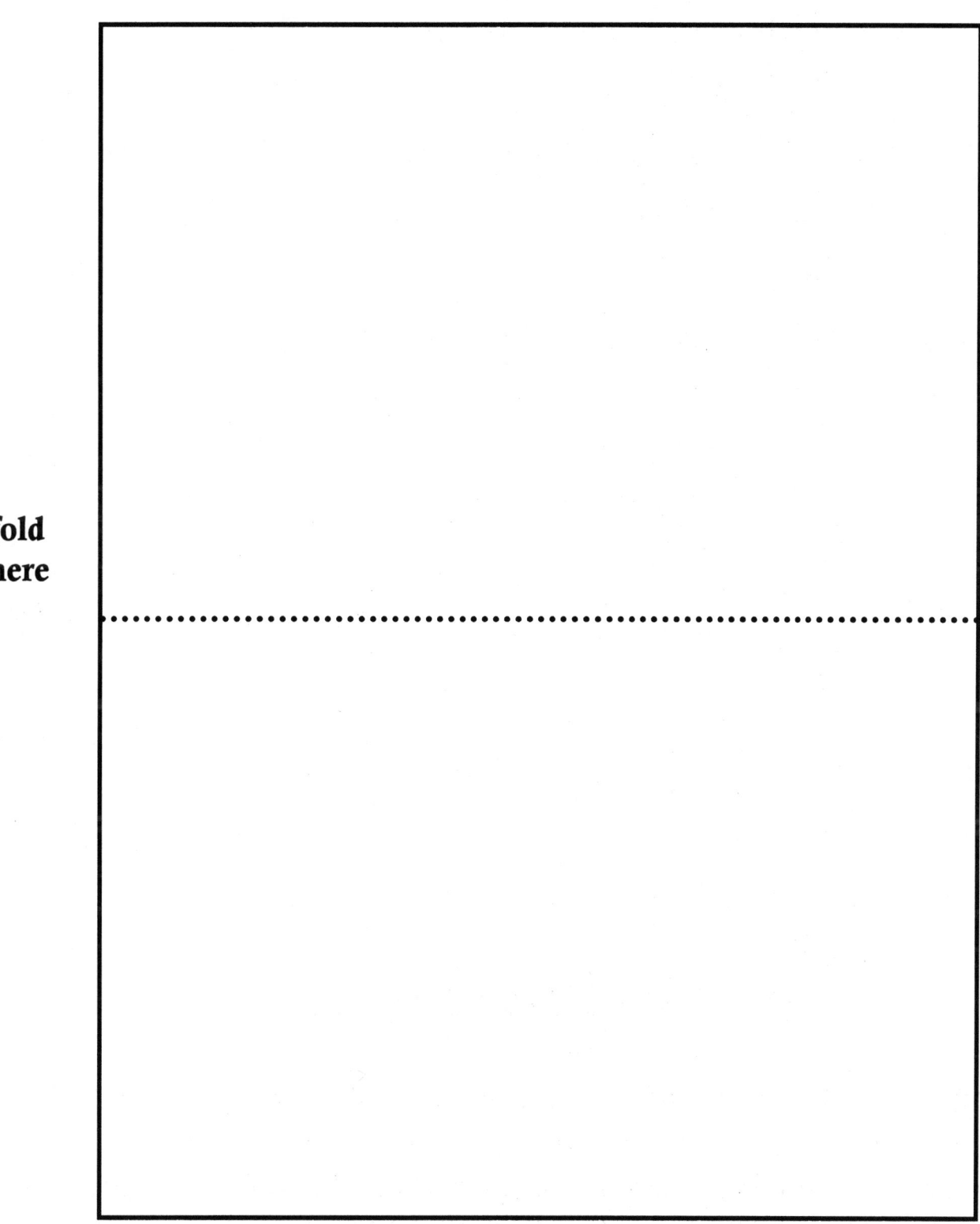

fold here

cut here

Thank You! *Thank You!*

Assignment: Color and cut out the clothes on page 93 and paste or glue them on your figures on page 61. Can you make some of your own clothes for them?

Let's Get Dressed!

Assignment: Let's make a birthday card. Use a lot of bright colors for this card. Do you want to color a clown on it? Do you remember how to draw balloons? Are you going to use some of your stickers? You can even cut out *Happy Birthday* to place on your card.

Happy Birthday! Happy Birthday!

cut here

fold here

···

cut here

Happy Birthday! **Happy Birthday!**

Assignment: Follow the instructions on page 97 to make some beautiful angels! Use the other long strip to create your own chain of figures.

Making Angels

A.

B.

1. We are going to use this paper lengthwise to give us a longer strip to make our chain of angels. First, cut out the long strip from top to bottom.

2. Fold this long strip of paper, like an accordion, where the light lines are drawn.

3. Cut out the angel on the front through all of the other folded sections. Make sure not to cut the tips of the wings or the corners of the robe!

4. Open it up and you have created a beautiful chain of angels.

5. Can you draw a chain of figures in box A? You may want to find a picture of a cuddly animal or cartoon character. Remember, let your characters connect at the borders of your paper so that you will be able to make a complete chain.

cut here

cut here

Assignment: As mentioned, for a *pop-up* card you can use a chain of figures gluing it to both sides of the card as explained on page 74.

A "Pop-Up" For Grandpop
cut here

fold here

cut here

Assignment: Let's make a *pop-up* card! It's just like making a regular card except for one little thing, it pops up when you open it. Have fun!

Assignment: Let's make another card, but this time we will make a collage! A collage is an artistic composition made up of various materials, like photographs and pictures. If you like, you can even add some of your dried flowers and stickers. Just glue them together in a creative way. Are you going to write a greeting?

Making a Photo Card

cut here

fold here

cut here

Assignment: Follow the instructions on page 76 to make a beautiful, pressed flower greeting card.

cut here

fold here

cut here

Let's Make a Pressed Flower Greeting Card!

Colored Markers

"Study to find thyself approved." Isaiah 28:10

Colored Markers

Now that you have finished, *"Little Annie's,"* it is time for your reward! We are going to use colored markers and learn how to color your "marker cards." Notice that the 5 marker cards are on a thick paper so that the colors will not seep through to the other side and the paper will not bubble up. Coloring with markers is fun! They have bright colors and you can do many delightful things, like coloring with dots, lines, or blending. One golden rule to remember is, *"Always put the tops back on the markers."*

Marker Card #1

Before beginning, we encourage you to follow these instructions and color in page 107 with your colored pencils. When finished, place *Marker Card #1* in front of you. First, color in the 3 pie shapes yellow, red and blue in the circle on the bottom left-hand corner of your marker card. These are called your *primary colors*. The circle is called a *color wheel* and teaches you how to use color in your pictures. When you have finished, take yellow dots and place them very close together in the pie shape that is in-between the yellow and the red. Next, take your red marker and add red dots real close together in-between the yellow dots. Yellow and red makes orange. This gives you an idea of how to mix your colors to create new colors. Then, color the pie shape in-between the red and the blue with red dots and blue dots. This will show you how to make purple, or violet. Finally, color in the pie shape in-between the blue and the yellow with yellow and blue dots to make green. Next, color in the three balloons in-between the two color wheels using any two colors you like for each balloon. Color with *dots* to create a new color for each. Coloring with dots is a delightful method, or technique, for coloring. *Remember, always keep your dots very close together.*

Color Me In

Color in the picture above with your colored pencils following the same instructions on pages 106 and 108. This will be good practice for you and show you how different colored pencils are from colored markers. The only thing is, you cannot paint with your pencils, so you will have to color in both the light blue sky and the light flesh tone for Annie.

107

Next, place a cup of water to the side of your marker card and take a brush and dip it in the water. Rub your wet brush in the blue pie shape of the color wheel and paint a light blue sky behind Annie. Do not color in the clouds, trees or balloons. Notice how light the blue is which you created for your sky!

Your *secondary colors* are orange, purple and green. Can you color in the color wheel in the bottom right-hand corner? Place the three primary colors yellow, red and blue in the same pie shapes as in your first color wheel. Then, take your orange colored marker and color in the pie shape in-between the yellow and the red, your purple in-between the red and the blue, and your green in-between the blue and the yellow. You have just completed your color wheel with both your primary and secondary colors. Dip your brush in water again and rub it in the orange pie shape. Then, paint a very light orange, or flesh tone on Annie's face, hands, and legs above her socks. Again, this is like beginning painting. Notice how light your flesh tone is. Before continuing, color in the balloons below with your colored pencils; 3 with your primary colors and 3 with your secondary colors.

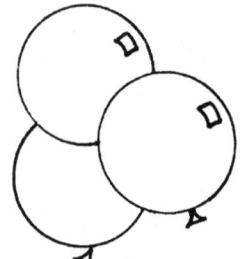

3 with Primary Colors

3 with Secondary Colors

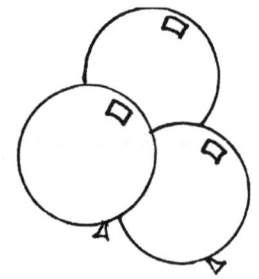

Next, color in Annie's bows in her hair and her apron (except for the polka dots) with your red colored marker. Color her hair, shoes and polka dots with your black marker. For the grass, use short yellow, green and blue vertical strokes. Keep these strokes very short and close together. This will create a nice, colorful, *"grassy"* effect.

short yellow,
blue
& green strokes

Finally, color in the rest of your picture anyway you like with your markers. Can you draw and color some nice designs in the border around Annie? You can draw anything you like! You may want to draw sunshines, flowers and leaves, half moons, stars, triangles, or even polka dots in the picture frame. You may want to color the flowers with dots by using yellow and red dots, or red and blue dots. Start your drawing lightly with a light colored pencil and then go over your designs with your colored markers.

Color Me In

Before using your colored markers for *Marker Card #2*, color in the picture above with your colored pencils following the instructions on page 110. This is good practice and will show you how different colored pencils are from colored markers.

Marker Card #2

   Place *Marker Card #2* in front of you. Before beginning, color in the picture on page 109 with your colored pencils using these same instructions. When you are finished, color in one of the hearts on the top of your marker card with your blue colored marker. Then, color in the other heart on the top of your marker card with your orange colored marker. Take your brush and wet it in a cup of water. Then, rub it in the blue heart and paint a light blue sky behind the little girl, her dog, and around the hearts. If you run out of color, dip your brush in water again and rub it in the blue heart one more time. Next, dip your brush in water and rub it in the orange heart, painting in the little girl's face, arms and legs with a very light orange, or flesh tone. You may also want to paint the flesh of the two baby angels with this light color; however, leave their wings white.

   Color in the grass with short vertical strokes with your yellow, blue and green colored markers just as you did in *Marker Lesson #1*. Remember, keep your strokes very short and very close together.

A.  Let's add some texture to the dog by using short strokes of orange and brown real close together as illustrated to the left (A). Practice this first on the puppy dog on the bottom of your *marker card*. First, make short orange strokes for his fur, and then add brown strokes. It is always good to put your lightest colors in before your darker colors. Next, color in his collar and tongue a bright red. *Remember, keep your strokes very short and very close together*. When you are finished, take your brown colored marker and color in short brown strokes over the orange strokes and you have just given your puppy dog a nice, colorful, *"furry"* coat.

   Color in the rest of your picture any way you like. You may want to color the flowers with dots. Color the leaves and the stems of the flowers yellow and green, and the little girl's hair yellow and her shoes brown. How would you like to color her dress and socks?

   Finally, draw some flowers in the two figure boxes on the bottom of your *marker card*. You may want to draw them with one of your colored pencils and then color over them with your markers. Can you draw petals for your flowers and a few leaves?

Color Me In

Annie's: *Marker Card #3*

Before using your colored markers, color in the picture above with your colored pencils following the same instructions as for *Marker Card #3* (page 112). Since you cannot paint with your pencils, you will have to color in a light blue area behind the sad clown and also a light flesh tone for the clowns skin with your orange or pink colored pencil.

Marker Card #3

*Happy faces up! Sad faces down....*Place *Marker Card #3* in front of you along with a brush and a cup of water. Today, we are going to color a happy clown and a sad clown. Do you know what your 3 *warm colors* are? They are yellow, red and orange. They look warm, don't they? Look at your markers again. Do you know what your 3 *cool colors* are? They are *blue, purple and green*. If you close your eyes, they almost feel cool, don't they? Warm colors seem bright and cheerful, whereas cool colors can sometimes seem sad and gloomy. We are going to color the happy clown with warm colors and the sad clown with cool colors.

To begin, color the 3 rectangles on the bottom left side of your *marker card*, using your 3 warm colors (yellow, red and orange). Then, color in the 3 rectangles on the right side with your 3 cool colors (blue, purple and green). Next, **dip your brush in water and rub it in the blue rectangle and paint a light blue background behind the sad clown on the top of your marker card.** Try to paint around the raindrops, keeping them white.

A.  Next, rub your wet brush in the orange rectangle and color the flesh of the clowns a light orange. However, **do not paint around the mouth. This areas always remains white (A).** Practice on the two clown faces in the middle of your *marker card*. *Up! Up! Up! & Down, Down, Down.*

Yes!   No!

Can you color in the 5 balloons on your *marker card* with your warm and cool colors, placing one color over another? However, this time let's practice coloring with *lines*. Color the first balloon with yellow vertical lines very close together. Make sure no white is showing in your balloon except for the little window, or *"highlight."* When you are finished, color blue vertical lines in-between the yellow lines. Color the remaining balloons with vertical lines, using first a warm color and then adding vertical lines in-between them with any cool color you like. See how many new colors you can create! *Remember, take your time and keep your lines very close together.* Then, color the rest of the happy clown with your warm colors and color the rest of the sad clown using your cool colors.

Color Me In

Annie's: *Marker Card #4*

Before using your colored markers for *Marker Card #4*, color in the picture above with your colored pencils following the same instructions as on page 114.

Marker Card #4

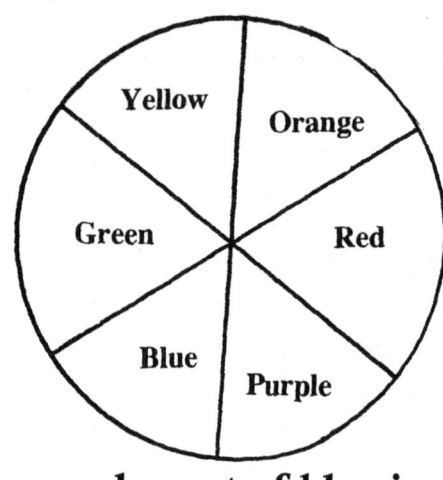

Let's place *Marker Card #4* in front of you. You have learned your primary and secondary colors. You have also learned warm and cool colors. On page 25, you learned about your complementary colors. Now, let's learn more about them. As you know, complementary colors are opposite each other on the color wheel. So, the complement of red is green, the complement of yellow is purple, and the complement of blue is orange.

First, color in the color wheel above with your colored pencils and then color the color wheel on the bottom of your *marker card* with your markers just as you did above. Again, notice that complementary colors are across from each other on your color wheel. Complementary colors also love to be next to each other in your pictures as they sing when they are together!

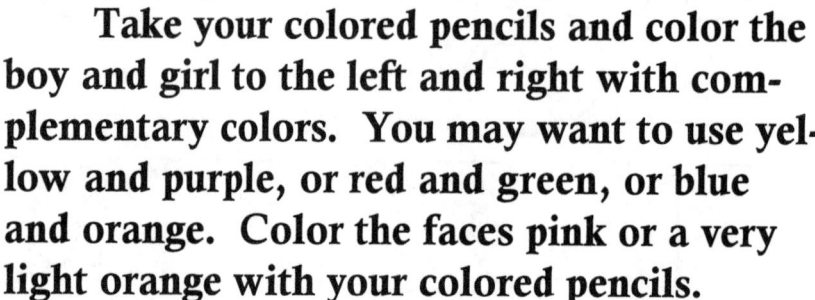

Take your colored pencils and color the boy and girl to the left and right with complementary colors. You may want to use yellow and purple, or red and green, or blue and orange. Color the faces pink or a very light orange with your colored pencils.

Now, take your colored markers and color the two jars on the bottom of your marker card with complementary colors. When finished, take your brush, wet it in a cup of water and rub it in the orange pie shape of your color wheel. Then, paint in the hands and faces of the three little figures with a light orange, or flesh tone. Color the hair of the three figures with either yellow, brown or orange. Color their shoes with your black or brown colored markers. Finally, color in the three figures' clothing using a different set of complementary colors for each, coloring one with red and green, one with yellow and purple, and one with blue and orange.

A.
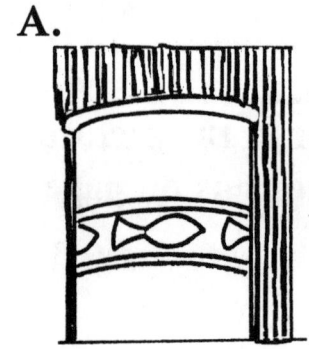

Last of all, let's color in the background of the shelves with long, controlled vertical lines, placing them close together (A). Use orange, red and purple vertical lines. *Remember, take your time.*

114

Color Me In

Annie's: *Marker Card #5*

My Masterpiece by: _____

Before doing *Marker Card #4*, color in the picture above with your colored pencils following the same instructions as on page 116. A nice way to make a flat color for your sky is by coloring with the side of your pencil point. Also, see if you can color your water with horizontal lines.

Marker Card #5

Today we are going to color in a beautiful sunset sky! Place *Marker Card #5* in front of you, and with your yellow marker, color your entire sky yellow. Please be careful to go around the clouds and the sailboat. Next, just above the sun and the sailboat, color a straight, horizontal band of orange going across your yellow sky. Next, color a band of red above the orange, then purple above the red, and a band of blue for the top part of your sky. When you are finished, take a wet brush and blend the colors together to make a beautiful sunset sky!

Color the sun with your yellow colored marker and also the sun's reflection in the water with yellow horizontal strokes (see below). Horizontal strokes are a good way to draw or color water as it helps to show the current or flow of the water (A). Next, take your orange colored marker and color over the yellow sun. Then, add orange horizontal strokes over the yellow horizontal strokes in the sun's reflection on the water. However, break your strokes occasionally to add a nice sparkle!

Add a Nice Sparkle to Your Water

A.

Color the water to either side of the sun's reflection first with green, broken horizontal lines, then with purple, broken horizontal lines and finally, with blue, broken horizontal lines. Color your palm tree and coconuts with orange and brown, the palm leaves with yellow and green, and the flower with yellow and orange. Do you know how to color the parts of the boy's hands, feet and face?

When you are finished, neatly print your name on the bottom of your picture.

*My Masterpiece by:*_____.

More Fun with Colored Markers

Here are some more assignments if you would like to have more fun with colored markers. You may also want to do some of the previous lessons in *Annie's* over again, but this time do the assignments with your markers. Don't forget to use a thick paper, like poster board or a card stock paper when using your markers. Have fun! Be creative and try to use some of the new techniques you have just learned.

Independent Lessons with Markers:

1. A Teddy Bear: Do you have a teddy bear or other stuffed animal? Place it in front of you and draw it lightly with your yellow colored pencil. Then, go over it with your orange and brown markers (or any colors you like) to show the texture of the fur. Make sure to use very short, close together strokes for the fur.

2. An Apple: Place a red apple in front of you. Draw it lightly with your yellow colored pencil and then go over it with your other colored markers. How many colors do you see in a red apple? Do you see some yellow, orange, purple and maybe even green? When you are finished, you may want to blend your colors together with a wet brush.

3. Daddy's Neckties: Aren't neckties colorful! Neatly place some of your father's neckties in front of you. For that matter, you can use any assortment of colorful fabric. See how creative and colorful you can become with your picture!

4. Coloring Like an Impressionist! Go to the library and take a book out on Vincent van Gogh or Claude Monet. Copy one of their pictures with your yellow colored pencil and then go over it with your colored markers, using bold colorful strokes!

5. Going Outside: Go outside and create pictures from nature. This can be very inspiring as you are in God's studio. Find something very simple to draw like one flower, one insect or a leaf. How many colors do you see? Draw it lightly with your yellow colored pencil and then color it in with your markers.

The End

It's Travel Time!

Pressed Patty   Flat Jack

Color *"Pressed Patty"* and *"Flat Jack"* with your colored pencils or markers and then cut them out. Give one to a friend and keep one for yourself. Have them travel with you and your friend for a week and tell all the good things that they did: the manners, the thoughtfulness, the proper etiquette, and so forth. Carry them in a protected pocket, a book or a convenient place. Write their good deeds below.

"Pressed Patty" "Flat Jack"	Day	Good Deeds

What Do We Recommend Next?

Now that you have finished Little Annie's Art Book Of Etiquette and Good Manners, How Great Thou ART Publications has many other delightful art books you may want to go to next. For example, if you are still a preschooler, we would recommend Baby Lamb's Book of Art, or Joseph the Canada Goose. If you are now over the age of five and really like art, then we would recommend I Can Do All Things. Below is a brief description of each.

Baby Lambs Book of ART   Ages 3 thru 5

Not a coloring book! Teaches beginning drawing and color theory with many fun and easy lessons for preschoolers. Also includes a section on lettering, addition and subtraction, beginning lettering and writing, cut and paste, stories from the Bible, games, ABCs with scripture, and 5 delightful "marker cards," all in a fun way with art! 128 pages of instruction.
A one year curriculum.

Ask about our Bundle Package
(recommended art supplies and text at a savings!)

Joseph the Canada Goose   Ages 4 thru 8

We hope you find this children's story and art book as delightful to read as we did creating it! This is the story of a Canada goose named Joseph with a broken wing, and his relationship with a lonely old farmer named Elmer Thatcher. What makes this book unique is that the pages contain art lessons to go along with the story. Text includes 100 pages with over 45 art lessons and many children's illustrations of Joseph.
A one year curriculum

Ask about our Bundle Package
(recommended art supplies and text at a savings!)

I Can Do All Things   Ages 6 & Up

A homeschoolers' favorite. I Can Do All Things is designed to teach younger children beginning drawing, painting and color theory. A best selling program with 225 pages containing courses in: beginning drawing, how to use colored markers, how to us colored pencils and beginning painting. Text also includes 38 paint cards (for the painting assignments) and a section titled "Studying the Masters," which is a great introduction to art history.
A 3 Year Curriculum

Ask about our Bundle Package
(recommended art supplies and text at a savings!)

Order Today! 1-800-982-DRAW (3729)

Art for all Ages!

From Pre-School to Adult

Beginning Drawing
Beginning Painting
Color Theory
Art History
Learn How to Use
Colored Pencils & Colored Markers

Videos & DVD's
Art Supplies
Time & Family Tested
Step-by-step Instruction
Daily Lessons
Satisfaction Guaranteed

Call today for more information: 800-982-DRAW (3729)
How Great Thou Art Publications
Box 48 McFarlan, N.C. 28102
email: sales@howgreatthouart.com   web site: www.howgreatthouart.com